Colorado Christian University
Library
180 S. Garrison
Lakewood, Colorado 80226

The Battle of Gettysburg

Other books in the At Issue in History series:

The Attack on Pearl Harbor
The Conquest of the New World
The Crash of 1929
The Cuban Missile Crisis
The Indian Reservation System
Japanese American Internment Camps
The Nuremberg Trials
The Sinking of the Titanic
The Treaty of Versailles

18.70

The
Battle of
Gettysburg

James Tackach, *Book Editor*

Daniel Leone, *President*
Bonnie Szumski, *Publisher*
Scott Barbour, *Managing Editor*

 OPPOSING
VIEWPOINTS® **AT ISSUE IN HISTORY**
SERIES

GREENHAVEN PRESS
SAN DIEGO, CALIFORNIA

GALE GROUP
™
THOMSON LEARNING
Detroit • New York • San Diego • San Francisco
Boston • New Haven, Conn. • Waterville, Maine
London • Munich

No part of this book may be reproduced or used in any form or by any means, electrical, mechanical, or otherwise, including, but not limited to, photocopy, recording, or any information storage and retrieval system, without prior written permission from the publisher.

Library of Congress Cataloging-in-Publication Data

The Battle of Gettysburg / James Tackach, book editor.
    p. cm. — (At issue in history)
    Includes bibliographical references and index.
    ISBN 0-7377-0817-4 (lib. : alk. paper). —
ISBN 0-7377-0816-6 (pbk. : alk. paper)
    1. Gettysburg (Pa.), Battle of, 1863. I. Tackach, James, 1953– . II. Series.

E475.53 B34 2002
973.7'349—dc21

                            2001040735

Cover photo: © Digital Stock
Library of Congress, 35, 43, 49, 73, 87, 109
National Archives, 67

Copyright © 2002 by Greenhaven Press,
an imprint of The Gale Group
10911 Technology Place, San Diego, CA 92127

Printed in the U.S.A.

Every effort has been made to trace owners of copyrighted material.

Contents

Chapter 3: Was the North's Victory at Gettysburg Incomplete?

Chapter 4: The Battle of Gettysburg in Context

Foreword

Historian Robert Weiss defines history simply as "a record and interpretation of past events." Both elements—record and interpretation—are necessary, Weiss argues.

> Names, dates, places, and events are the essence of history. But historical writing is not a compendium of facts. It consists of facts placed in a sequence to tell a connected story. A work of history is not merely a story, however. It also must analyze what happened and *why*—that is, it must interpret the past for the reader.

For example, the events of December 7, 1941, that led President Franklin D. Roosevelt to call it "a date which will live in infamy" are fairly well known and straightforward. A force of Japanese planes and submarines launched a torpedo and bombing attack on American military targets in Pearl Harbor, Hawaii. The surprise assault sank five battleships, disabled or sank fourteen additional ships, and left almost twenty-four hundred American soldiers and sailors dead. On the following day, the United States formally entered World War II when Congress declared war on Japan.

These facts and consequences were almost immediately communicated to the American people who heard reports about Pearl Harbor and President Roosevelt's response on the radio. All realized that this was an important and pivotal event in American and world history. Yet the news from Pearl Harbor raised many unanswered questions. Why did Japan decide to launch such an offensive? Why were the attackers so successful in catching America by surprise? What did the attack reveal about the two nations, their people, and their leadership? What were its causes, and what were its effects? Political leaders, academic historians, and students look to learn the basic facts of historical events and to read the intepretations of these events by many different sources, both primary and secondary, in order to develop a more complete picture of the event in a historical context.

In the case of Pearl Harbor, several important questions surrounding the event remain in dispute, most notably the role of President Roosevelt. Some historians have blamed his policies for deliberately provoking Japan to attack in order to propel America into World War II; a few have gone so far as to accuse him of knowing of the impending attack but not informing others. Other historians, examining the same event, have exonerated the president of such charges, arguing that the historical evidence does not support such a theory.

The Greenhaven At Issue in History series recognizes that many important historical events have been interpreted differently and in some cases remain shrouded in controversy. Each volume features a collection of articles that focus on a topic that has sparked controversy among eyewitnesses, contemporary observers, and historians. An introductory essay sets the stage for each topic by presenting background and context. Several chapters then examine different facets of the subject at hand with readings chosen for their diversity of opinion. Each selection is preceded by a summary of the author's main points and conclusions. A bibliography is included for those students interested in pursuing further research. An annotated table of contents and thorough index help readers to quickly locate material of interest. Taken together, the contents of each of the volumes in the Greenhaven At Issue in History series will help students become more discriminating and thoughtful readers of history.

Introduction
Gettysburg: Victory and Controversy

The essential facts of the Battle of Gettysburg are not at issue. On the first three days of July in 1863, on the ridges, in the woods, and on the farm fields outside of the small town of Gettysburg, Pennsylvania, the Army of Northern Virginia, commanded by Confederate general Robert E. Lee, and the Army of the Potomac, led by Union general George Meade, waged the greatest battle of the Civil War, and perhaps even the greatest battle in American history. During three days of furious fighting, Lee's army, which comprised 75,000 men as it marched into Pennsylvania, lost 28,000 men. Meade's army, which began the battle with about 90,000 men, suffered 23,000 casualties. On July 4, General Lee's badly wounded army began a slow retreat southward toward Virginia.

Also not at issue is the severity of the combat. Though a veteran of a bloody battle at Shiloh, Antietam, Fredericksburg, Chickamauga, or Cold Harbor might claim to have endured a crueler test on the battlefield than the soldier at Gettysburg, the fighting at Gettysburg was warfare at its worst. The battle featured substantial artillery bombardment, fierce hand-to-hand fighting, and infantry charges over open fields directly into artillery and infantry set in well-entrenched defensive positions. A Union private who had participated in the fierce fighting for the heights at Little Round Top on the second day of combat remembered "the screaming and bursting of shells, canister and shrapnel as they tore through the struggling masses of humanity, the death screams of wounded animals, the groans of their human companions, wounded and dying . . . —a perfect hell on earth, never, perhaps to be equaled, certainly not to be surpassed, nor *ever* to be forgotten in a man's lifetime."[1] A journalist covering the battle described the Confederate advance into the center of the Union defenses on the final day of combat in similarly horrific terms: "The lines have disappeared like a straw in a candle's flame. The ground is thick with dead, and the wounded are like the withered leaves of autumn."[2]

At issue, however, is almost everything else about the great battle—the wisdom of General Lee's Pennsylvania campaign, his battle strategy and tactics, and the Union movements in the aftermath of the battle. In the hands of Civil War and military historians, the Battle of Gettysburg has come to resemble a complicated and controversial literary text that critics continue to explore and debate.

Lee's Pennsylvania Campaign

In mid-May of 1863, Confederate president Jefferson Davis conferred with his top generals and military advisors to decide on a war plan for the coming summer. General Lee had just engineered a brilliant victory over the Army of the Potomac at Chancellorsville, and the Union army was not immediately threatening Lee's troops in Virginia. Davis's Secretary of War, James Seddon, suggested that a portion of Lee's army remain in Virginia to defend Richmond, the Confederate capital, while a corps under the command of General James Longstreet march toward Vicksburg, Mississippi, to reinforce a Confederate army that was receiving pressure from Union troops directed by General Ulysses S. Grant. Confederate general P.G.T. Beauregard recommended that Lee begin an offensive in Tennessee, which might prompt Grant to abandon his Vicksburg campaign to fight Lee. Lee, however, proposed a more daring plan—an invasion of Pennsylvania.

Lee had planned an invasion of Pennsylvania earlier in the war, in September 1862, but his advance was checked by the Army of the Potomac near Antietam Creek in Sharpsburg, Maryland. The Battle of Antietam, fought on September 17, 1862, was the bloodiest single day of fighting of the Civil War. Lee lost almost 11,000 men, and the Union army with which he clashed lost more than 12,000. After that engagement, Lee abandoned his plan for an invasion of the North and returned to Virginia.

In May of 1863, however, Lee was confident that his army could push into Pennsylvania, defeat the Army of the Potomac on Northern soil, and perhaps take control of a

major Northern city such as Baltimore or Philadelphia. If that plan worked, President Abraham Lincoln would be pressured to come to the peace table and recognize the South's independence, ending the war. If the Army of the Potomac refused to fight Lee in Pennsylvania, Lee's troops could, at least, live off Union land for a time, relieving Virginia of the burden of supplying the Confederate army with food. President Davis accepted Lee's suggestion, and Lee began to move his army northward in early June.

Historians continue to debate the wisdom of Lee's plan. Before this daring invasion of the North, Lee had succeeded in holding the larger Army of the Potomac to a stalemate by waging, for the most part, a defensive war. He had smashed advancing Union armies twice at Bull Run, in July 1861 and again in late August 1862. He had foiled Union general George McClellan's Peninsular Campaign of spring 1862. He had routed Union advances at Fredericksburg in December 1862 and at Chancellorsville in early May 1863. Many Civil War historians argue that Lee would have been wise to remain in Virginia and allow the Union army to attack him once again, rather than to invade Union soil for a second time. "Was there an alternative to Lee's glorious campaign leading to total defeat?" asks Lee biographer Alan T. Nolan. In Nolan's view, there was: "a defensive grand strategy, within the context of which Lee could on occasion have undertaken offensive threats, appropriate operationally strategic and tactical offensives."[3]

On June 3, 1863, however, Lee began to move his army northward. His troops marched west of Virginia's Blue Ridge Mountains, through Maryland, and into the rich farmlands of southern Pennsylvania. When he received reports of Lee's troop movements, General Meade began moving his Army of the Potomac northward from their camps near Frederick, Maryland. Meade made sure to keep his army positioned between Lee's troops and Washington, D.C.

But Lee was unaware of Meade's movements. Lee's cavalry, under the command of General J.E.B. Stuart, was supposed to place itself between Lee's infantry and Meade's troops. Instead, Stuart's horsemen had ridden completely around Meade's men, and Stuart could not quickly get word to Lee when Meade's army began to move. In late June, Lee, believing that Meade remained encamped in Maryland, spread his troops thinly along a forty-five mile crescent north of the small town of Gettysburg. He was not prepared for a major battle.

The First Day of Fighting

On the morning of July 1, Meade sent toward Gettysburg a division of cavalry under the command of General John Buford to scout Lee's position and a large infantry force under General John Reynolds to support Buford if fighting broke out. It did. Buford's cavalry ran into Lee's troops west of Gettysburg. His troops dismounted and faced Lee's men along a ridge west of town. Lee, surprised by the arrival of Meade's men, immediately ordered his thinly spread army to concentrate at Gettysburg, where a furious fight was erupting. Reynolds's infantry had arrived to support Buford's cavalry, but advancing Confederate troops pushed them back toward and through the town. Reynolds was killed, and his replacement, General Winfield Hancock, rallied the retreating Union troops on high ground just south of Gettysburg, a position that Meade agreed could and must be held.

By the evening of the first day of combat, Meade had stretched his men in a line of defense shaped like an upside-down fishhook on high ground known as Cemetery Ridge between two elevations, Culp's Hill on the north and the Little Round Top on the south. Lee placed his men north and west of the large Union army and then consulted with his

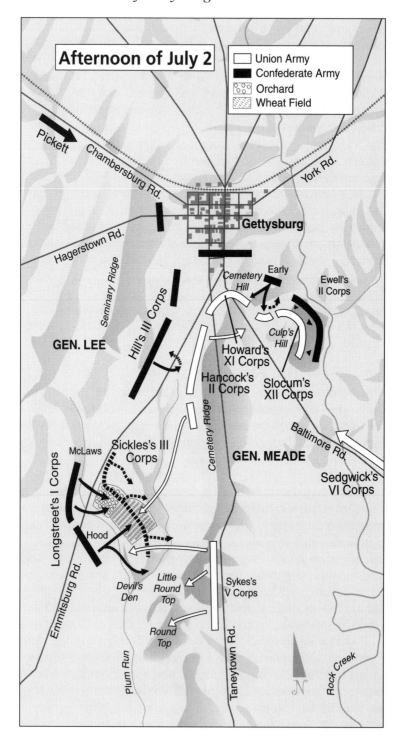

generals on how and where he would launch an attack. Lee's top general, James Longstreet, advised Lee to reposition his army south of Meade's men and force Meade to attack. But Lee wished to take the offensive. He planned to send Longstreet's troops toward Little Round Top on Meade's southern flank, then attack Meade's center and northern flank if Meade reinforced his troops on Little Round Top.

The Second Day

Longstreet was supposed to make his attack in the early afternoon, but his troops moved slowly and were not ready for an assault until four o'clock—a delay that prompts some historians to blame Longstreet for the South's ultimate defeat. Longstreet's attack, when it finally came, was furious. Bitter fighting exploded on the Little and Big Round Tops and below them in a wheat field and peach orchard. Longstreet almost turned the Union flank, but a regiment of Maine troops, commanded by Colonel Joshua Lawrence Chamberlain, stubbornly held their ground on the Little Round Top despite repeated Rebel assaults. The attack on Meade's north and center also developed late—around dusk—and it, too, was repulsed.

After two days of hard fighting, with heavy casualties on both sides, the battle was essentially a stalemate. Lee's troops had valiantly attempted and failed to puncture the Union lines. Meade had fought off but not defeated Lee's army.

The Third Day

On the morning of July 3, Lee made his most daring and controversial decision of the Gettysburg campaign. Longstreet again advised Lee to move around Meade's southern flank and attack him from the rear, but Lee had decided upon a full-force attack on the center of Meade's line that was entrenched in strong positions along Cemetery Ridge. He named General George Pickett to lead the attack. By this time, Stuart's cavalry had returned, and Lee ordered Stuart's troops to circle around the Union southern flank and strike Meade from behind.

At around one o'clock Confederate artillery erupted. Lee wanted to soften Meade's center with a significant artillery bombardment before Pickett's attack, but most of the Rebel batteries overshot their mark, hitting reserve troops, officers' headquarters, and field hospitals behind Meade's lines. Meade answered with an artillery barrage of his own, and citizens as far away as eastern Ohio claimed to have heard the guns of Gettysburg that afternoon. The cannons eventually ceased firing, and 14,000 Confederate troops emerged from the woods to the west of Cemetery Ridge and commenced a quick march over an open field a mile or so wide toward the center of Meade's line.

Exposed in an open field to Union artillery and infantry fire, Pickett's troops were cut to pieces. More than half of Pickett's 14,000 men were killed, wounded, or captured. Pickett's infantry reached the Union line in only one place, near a clump of trees at the very center of Cemetery Ridge, but the Confederates could neither puncture Meade's defenses nor hold their ground. The Confederate survivors began a quick retreat across the open field across which they had just marched. Meanwhile, Union cavalry had repulsed Stuart's troops as they tried to outflank the line. The Union defenses had held.

As Pickett's beaten and bedraggled Confederates rejoined Lee's lines, Lee greeted them saying, "It was all my fault." He ordered Pickett to reform his division and prepare for a Union counterattack, but Pickett responded, "General Lee, I *have* no division now."[4] Longstreet, who vehemently opposed Lee's tactics on the third day, reportedly later told Lee, "General Lee, there was never a body of fifteen thousand men who could make that attack successfully."[5] The day after Pickett's charge failed, Lee began to withdraw his troops from Pennsylvania, keeping a rear guard ready to repel any Union attack, and leaving thousands of wounded and dying soldiers behind.

The Aftermath of the Battle

Meade excitedly reported a Union victory to Washington. He had stopped Lee's invasion of Pennsylvania and inflicted heavy losses on the Confederate army. But President Abraham Lincoln wanted more; he urged Meade to attack Lee and destroy the Army of Northern Virginia. Lincoln had just learned of Grant's victory at Vicksburg, and the president reasoned that a death blow to Lee's army could end the war.

Meade followed Lee but did not attack him. When he expressed satisfaction with driving Lee's army from Northern soil, the frustrated Lincoln responded, "Will our gener-

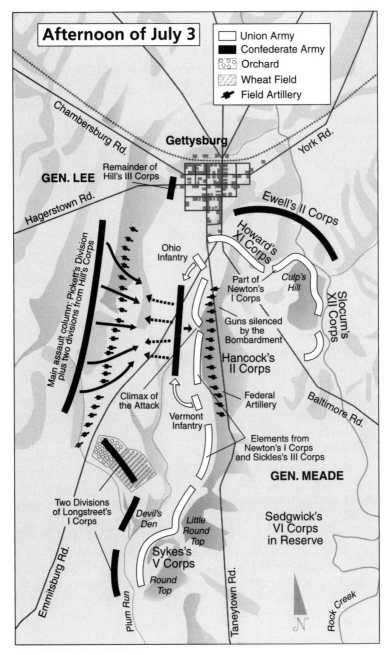

Afternoon of July 3

- Union Army
- Confederate Army
- Orchard
- Wheat Field
- Field Artillery

Chambersburg Rd.

Gettysburg

York Rd.

GEN. LEE

Remainder of Hill's III Corps

Hagerstown Rd.

Ewell's II Corps

Howard's XI Corps

Ohio Infantry

Main assault column: Pickett's Division plus two divisions from Hill's Corps

Part of Newton's I Corps

Culp's Hill

Slocum's XII Corps

Guns silenced by the Bombardment

Hancock's II Corps

Climax of the Attack

Vermont Infantry

Federal Artillery

Baltimore Rd.

Elements from Newton's I Corps and Sickles's III Corps

GEN. MEADE

Two Divisions of Longstreet's I Corps

Devil's Den

Little Round Top

Sedgwick's VI Corps in Reserve

Emmitsburg Rd.

Plum Run

Sykes's V Corps

Round Top

Taneytown Rd.

Rock Creek

N

als never get that idea out of their heads? The whole country is our soil."[6] The swollen Potomac River slowed Lee's retreat to Virginia, but Meade never ordered an attack—an indecision that brought Lincoln's wrath and the criticism of

Civil War historians. On July 13 and 14, Lee crossed the Potomac River into Virginia, ending the Gettysburg campaign.

Lee accepted responsibility for the Confederate defeat at Gettysburg and offered President Davis his resignation, which Davis immediately declined. Meade, hearing of Lincoln's anger, offered his resignation, which Lincoln promptly refused. Both generals would fight again, and the great civil war would continue for another twenty-one months. But the Union victory at Gettysburg had turned the tide of the war. In November 1863, Lincoln, speaking at the dedication of a memorial cemetery at Gettysburg, extolled the valor of the Union soldiers, who, in Lincoln's words, fought to give their nation "a new birth of freedom."[7] Writing after the war, Jefferson Davis expressed his belief that a Confederate victory at Gettysburg "would have ended the war."[8]

Notes

1. Geoffrey C. Ward, Ric Burns, and Ken Burns, *The Civil War: An Illustrated History*. New York: Alfred A. Knopf, 1990, p. 225.
2. Richard Wheeler, *Voices of the Civil War*. New York: Thomas Y. Crowell, 1976, p. 323.
3. Alan T. Nolan, *Lee Considered: General Robert E. Lee and Civil War History*. Chapel Hill: University of North Carolina Press, 1991, p. 100.
4. Ward, Burns, and Burns, pp. 235–36.
5. James M. McPherson, *Battle Cry of Freedom: The Civil War Era*. New York: Oxford University Press, p. 661.
6. Bruce Catton, *Gettysburg: The Final Fury*. Garden City, New York: Doubleday, 1974, p. 101.
7. Roy P. Basler, *The Collected Works of Abraham Lincoln*. Vol. VII. New Brunswick, New Jersey: Rutgers University Press, 1953, p. 23.
8. Jefferson Davis, *The Rise and Fall of the Confederate Government*. Vol. II. Cranbury, New Jersey: Thomas Yoseloff, 1958, p. 448.

Chapter 1

The Fury of the Battle

1

A Union Soldier Remembers Gettysburg

Robert Goldthwaite Carter

Robert Goldthwaite Carter, a Maine native, was a member of the 22nd Massachusetts infantry when he fought at Gettysburg. He survived the battle and the war and later attended and graduated from the United States Military Academy. During the 1890s, he used his own wartime letters and those of his three brothers, who also fought in the Union army, to write a series of articles for the *Maine Bugle*. In 1913, Carter collected his articles in a book titled *Four Brothers in Blue*. The excerpt from *Four Brothers in Blue* presented here describes the fierce fighting near the Little and Big Round Tops on the second day of battle. With these two hills at their back, Carter's regiment participated in the struggle in the wheat field and peach orchard near the Union army's southern flank.

"Fix bayonets!" rang through the woods—no other command. A shot, one, two, three, and then with a perfectly startling rattle and roar, the line blazed forth, followed by an incessant cheer that seemed to thrill to one's very marrow. The battle was on—the battle of the Fifth Corps, to save the position from which the Third Corps had been driven. Many, placing a heap of cartridges and caps on the ground in front of them, were soon busily engaged loading and firing as rapidly as possible. The discordant screeches and exultant yells of the grey-coated "Johnnies" rose high above the din and noise about us, instantly followed by our hearty, steady, solid cheers.

Excerpted from *Four Brothers in Blue*, by Robert Goldthwaite Carter (Austin: University of Texas Press, 1978).

The Confederates Attack

Across the run, the indistinct form of masses of men, presenting the usual, dirty, greyish, irregular line, were dimly visible and moving up with defiant yells, while here and there the cross-barred Confederate battle flags were plainly to be seen. Nearer and nearer came the charging masses. There seemed to be nothing on our minds but a strong, resolute desire to check the living torrents and a slight tendency to doubt oneself, when the bullets buzzed so closely by without touching some part of the body.

There was mingled with this thought, however, an occasional flash of sadness, as the pain-stamped face of some dying man was presented to view, when carried hurriedly to the rear. So much pain, yelling, and cheering, however, kept the leading ideas uppermost, and if any man had sensations of fear before or while going in, he had no time or opportunity for such thoughts now, and the loading and firing, the cheering and yelling, wholly engrossed every animated, human machine.

We had marched too far and borne too much to be pushed over the ridge. Now came the groans of the bullet-stricken wounded. Nothing was seen but the heavy clouds of smoke which the still air hardly stirred. The green leaves and twigs overhead fell in a constant shower, as they were clipped by the singing bullets.

The first man struck in the regiment was in our company, Charles Phillips, a Bradford boy; he was next on the writer's left in the front rank; a thud, a sickening, dull cracking sound and his head—his face streaming blood which filled his eyes and nose and gurgled in his mouth—fell upon the writer's left shoe. . . . The writer ceased firing for a brief moment to seize our comrade and lay him quietly on his back—the days had gone by when two men could leave the ranks to carry one wounded man to the rear—and then went on with his duty.

These are hasty reflections. We were not there long. [General John] Hood's Division, [General James] Longstreet's Corps ([General Lafayette] McLaw[s] now commanding, Hood having been wounded early in the charge), had charged, and swinging into this gap left between the two corps (Third and Fifth), soon doubled back the right and left, and with exultant yells had pressed around and overlapped us. We were *flanked.* The command "Change front to the rear by the right flank!" was passed along the line, for no orders by voice or bugle could now be heard above the roar and din of battle. We knew what it meant. It was not executed tactically, nor can such an order be under conditions of battle, for the tactical units being continually destroyed, the file closers and guides being killed or wounded, it is impossible to restore such units under such a fire. The command *"About face!"* was given, and our veterans without further orders proceeded to execute this most difficult tactical maneuver in the face of a most terrific fire. While passing out of the Rose's woods into the "Wheat Field," we moved through a division of the Second Corps (Caldwell's) which had been sent to fill a gap to our left, and were moving by their left flank. We were soon almost inextricably mixed up with them, and subjected to a terrible cross fire. . . .

No military reader can fail to see what the effect must have been on a brigade changing front to the rear by the right flank, in the midst of a fierce charge by many lines of battle massed, and meeting a division, closed *en masse,* marching by the left flank. And yet the Twenty-second coolly picked up their cartridges and percussion caps, carried all their wounded out on blankets, and even the latter's guns to the rear.

As we emerged from Rose's woods into the open swale or pasture, then the "Wheat Field," studded here and there with large boulders and stone walls which time has not changed, we shook ourselves clear of our Second Corps brothers and still moved in ordinary quick time. At this point, the northwest angle of the former wheat field, the lane connecting the Taneytown and Emmittsburg roads, divides this wood from Trostle's farm, and the land rises rather abruptly to the northwest, terminating in a plateau, or open, roomy ridge. On the north of the lane, at this point, there is also a piece of thin woods, leaving an open space a little over 150 yards in width. Here the rebels were pouring through—Kershaw's and Wofford's Brigades.

When coming out of the woods I saw two of our sergeants (Abbott and Hazeltine, for we had no ambulance men or stretcher carriers on *that line*) carrying a writhing form in a blanket, their rifles acting as carriers or bars. It proved to be quaint John Morrison. I could hear his pleading: "Oh, let me down to rest! Oh! I can stand it no longer!

Let me die!" He was shot through the bowels. As they rested him on the ground for a moment and he heard the yells of the oncoming enemy, he would feebly say: "Oh, take me up, Charlie (Hazeltine) don't let them get me!" and so he passed out of our sight to the rear to a strange Division Field Hospital (Eleventh Corps, near George Spangler's house), and there died. . . .

Fighting in the Peach Orchard

We had fallen back a few hundred yards, faced about and were now fronting this gap or elbow between the two corps (Third and Fifth) toward the peach orchard, and were soon firing northwest. We had been firing southwest. Although our line was somewhat broken or irregular, every man kept his eyes on the colors and each company organization, although depleted, was complete. Pandemonium now reigned. There was a horrible din, and for a few moments the uproar and confusion were appalling. The scene beggars description. The hand palsies, the tongue grows silent, as we attempt to portray the awful tragedy of this hour. All was confusion, noise, flashes, smoke, and deafening explosions. Cheers, yells, shrieks and groans, one incessant flash and roar of artillery (two batteries were within fifty yards of us), one ceaseless rolling and crackling of musketry. The solid, ringing cheers of the men in blue, the peculiar, high-pitched and unpleasant yells of the men in grey, rose above the din.

Generals, colonels, aids and orderlies galloped about through the smoke. The hoarse and indistinguishable order of commanding officers, the screaming and bursting of shells, canister and shrapnel with their swishing sound as they tore through the struggling masses of humanity, the death screams of wounded animals, the groans of their human companions, wounded and dying and trampled under foot by hurrying batteries, riderless horses and the moving lines of battle, all combined in an indescribable roar of discordant elements—in fact, a perfect hell on earth, never, perhaps, to be equalled, certainly not to be surpassed, nor *ever* to be forgotten in a man's lifetime. It has never been effaced from my memory, day or night, for fifty years. It was grim-visaged war, with all its unalterable horror, implacable, unyielding, full of sorrow, heart breaks, untold sufferings, wretched longings, doubts and fears.

As already stated, to our left as we faced when changing front in the elbow between the two corps and in the direction of the "Peach Orchard," directly in the gap, were Phillip's and Bigelow's Massachusetts Batteries. General Barnes and staff and Colonel W.S. Tilton, commanding our First Brigade, were here also. The fire of shot and shell through this breach and across our line had become, if possible, more terrific. Here General Barnes was wounded, Colonel Tilton of our own regiment had his horse shot, and Lieut. Walter Davis of the Twenty-Second, who was on General Barnes' staff, had the rim of his hat carried away.

Nothing could live before such a fire. The horses and many of the men of the batteries were shot away while bravely struggling to check the onward rush of the rebel masses. The rapid flashes and incessant peals from the guns of those two batteries told truthfully that the awful work allotted to them was being well performed, and the desperate bravery of these gallant cannoneers in that fearful breach can never receive too much praise. Bigelow was fighting, retiring with prolonge ropes attached. Lieut.-Col. F. McGilvery, Chief of Artillery of the First Volunteer Brigade of the Artillery Reserve, had ordered him to hold that point at all hazards. In the midst of the smoke, we could plainly see the cannoneers using their pistols, handspikes and sponge-staffs. He lost three officers, twenty-eight men and over eighty horses. The Eighth South Carolina, forming the left of Kershaw's Brigade, was the regiment that went directly in among Bigelow's guns, followed by some of Wofford's Georgia Brigade. The battery was practically captured at one time—four guns being abandoned to the enemy, all of which were subsequently brought off that night by Capt. Ed Dow, commanding the Sixth Maine Battery, who used his gun teams for that purpose. This is taken from Captain Bigelow and Captain Dow's own statement to the writer. He (Bigelow) was taken off the field supposed to be in a dying condition, but subsequently recovered. The battery expended three tons of shot and shell, including ninety-two rounds of canister, firing in all five hundred and twenty-eight rounds. Two other officers were killed, six out of seven sergeants were killed and wounded (two killed), seven corporals and twelve privates were killed and wounded and two taken prisoners. The enemy were standing in among and on the limber chests of Lieutenant Melton's section. Private

Ligal brained with a rammer head a Confederate who tried to capture him. The statistics of the War Department show that, with the single exception of a battery captured by a sudden charge at Iuka, Miss., it sustained the heaviest losses of any light battery in any single engagement of the whole war. We fell back through the "Wheat Field," Colonel Jeffords, of the Fourth Michigan, Second Brigade, being bayonetted while trying to save his colors just to our left. Standing waist deep in the beautiful yellow grain, the blue strongly contrasting, was the Regular Division, Gen. Romeyn B. Ayres commanding, dealing sledge-hammer blows. It was moving through the wheat field in column of battalions, close *en masse*, but marching as steadily as upon parade. They were delivering volleys from the front line, and the contrast of the tall yellow grain, so soon to be trampled by the succeeding columns, was very striking, and a scene never to be forgotten. Ayres had struck the enemy in flank as they were closely following our change of front through Rose's woods, had doubled them up and driven them back, but was in turn outflanked from the direction of the Devil's Den to the south. A large body of the enemy had gained his left rear, and facing about as we passed, he fought his way through and into our lines before dark, with a loss of more than half his force. As we were slowly falling back, firing as we went, "Here," said an officer of another company, a little panicky, and somewhat separated from his own men, to the writer, "Where is your company?" "Let that boy alone!" said our captain (J.H. Baxter), but a few feet distant, *"he knows what he is about!"* So did we all! For every man was intent upon preserving the regimental organization, and doing his entire duty. This officer proved to be the one whom our brother had driven back to the lines on the night of May 4 at [the Battle of] Chancellorsville, when the pickets flushed, and he was sprinting for the rifle pits in the moonlight.

Col. Thomas Sherwin, commanding our regiment, was seen to fall on his knees, just after crossing the low stone wall . . . as though shot through the body. Several sprang forward to assist him, but he immediately rose to his feet. A bullet had passed through his clothing and grazed his breast, without wounding him, but with sufficient force to knock him down. We halted at the foot, and on the northwest slope of Little Round Top. Eustis's Brigade of the Sixth

Corps was coming up and forming line of battle, about three to five hundred yards to our right. The uproar and confusion lulled. The Confederates came charging into our lines, and we captured many of Wofford's Brigade at this period. One "Johnny" had got in advance of their line, the charge having already spent itself like a huge wave upon the ocean beach, and they were much scattered. He was unattended and directly in front of the Eighteenth Massachusetts. The situation was ludicrous. "Hello, Johnny!" came from our boys, "you aren't going to capture us all alone, are you?" *He came in.* Many incidents could be related which have never been told of this afternoon's battle.

The shades of night gathered; only a few scattered shots could be heard, which, with the groans of the wounded, the cries for water, and the hum of thousands now lying on their arms as each related his experiences of the day, made a contrast to the fury of an hour before that was almost painful, and the reaction and the relaxation of the tense nerves almost prostrating. A tall Georgia sergeant, bare-headed—his coal black hair and fine features just visible in the gathering dusk—stepped over our prostrate bodies, and a voice cried out to the prisoner, "Going to the rear, Johnny?" "Yes, and I'm right glad to go to the *rare!*" We threw ourselves upon the ground, well wrapped up in a half blanket as a protection from the cold dew, and with a canteen for a pillow, we soon lost in peaceful slumber all remembrance of the perilous movements and the exciting details of the struggle which has been so imperfectly described.

2

A Confederate Soldier Remembers Gettysburg

Edmund DeWitt Patterson, an Ohio native living in Alabama, joined the Confederate army when the Civil War erupted in 1861. At Gettysburg, he fought with the 9th Alabama infantry and participated in General James Longstreet's unsuccessful attack on the Little Round Top on July 2. During the war, Patterson kept a journal that was preserved by his grandson, Edmund Brooks Patterson of West Newton, Massachusetts. In 1966, John G. Barrett of the Virginia Military Institute published Patterson's journal under the title *Yankee Rebel: The Civil War Journal of Edmund DeWitt Patterson*. Patterson's text describes camp life; Patterson's participation in battles at Bull Run, Fredericksburg, and Gettysburg; and life in a Union prisoner-of-war camp. This excerpt from *Yankee Rebel* describes the 9th Alabama's assault on the Little Round Top on the second day of combat at Gettysburg. Patterson's regiment is repulsed in furious fighting by stalwart Union troops, and Patterson is captured during the retreat. Patterson spent the remainder of the war in a prisoner-of-war camp on an island in Lake Erie.

The morning of the 2nd of July 1863 dawned on thousands of as brave hearts as were gathered together to battle for the right. And as the glorious sun rose in all his splendor shedding his rays on every hill top and flooding the Earth with light, the booming of artillery told us that all was not quiet along the lines, and that we had work before

Excerpted from *Yankee Rebel: The Civil War Journal of Edmund DeWitt Patterson*, edited by John G. Barrett (Chapel Hill: The University of North Carolina Press, 1966). Copyright © 1966 by The University of North Carolina Press. Reprinted with permission.

us. We had marched from Fayetteville the day before and had lain in line of battle all night protecting the extreme right flank of the army.

Assaulting the Union Lines

There had been hard fighting on the 1st and we well knew that one day's work could not decide the contest between two such powerful armies as now lay confronting each other near Gettysburg. Our noble army, flushed with a long series of brilliant victories and feeling unlimited confidence in the ability of General Lee and the justice of the cause for which we were fighting, were eager for the fray. We were soon in motion and with our gallant Wilcox at the head of the column were moving forward toward the center of the line of battle which was to be our position for the day. After marching some distance, we were ordered to halt, load our pieces and throw forward a skirmish line. We soon found our battle line, with the 10th and 11th Alabama Regiments a little in advance. These two regiments soon became hotly engaged with the enemy's sharpshooters, who were well posted behind a stone wall and in a strip of woods, but our boys soon succeeded in dislodging them, and our whole line moved forward and took position behind the stone fence from which we had just driven the enemy. During the little skirmish which lasted but a few moments, Maj. Fletcher and quite a number of others from the 8th, 10th, and 11th were wounded and a few killed.

As soon as our regiment got into position, our company was ordered forward as skirmishers, Cannon commanding the 1st platoon, I the second and Crow in command of the whole. I immediately moved forward in obedience to the orders and formed line with the Fla. skirmishers on my left, and my right resting at a large barn which afforded considerable protection to my men and was also a good lookout. We immediately opened fire on the enemy's line of sharpshooters and succeeded in making them withdraw some distance and causing some of the more daring, or obstinate ones, to bite the dust, and this too without any loss on our side. We remained at the barn for some time and until the Yankees brought a battery to bear upon it, when I withdrew the men, placing them on line with the rest of the company.

We, however, still kept a lookout at the place, and about three o'clock in the evening I noticed battery after battery and brigade after brigade being moved up to our right and we knew that something of interest was soon to take place in that direction, and we were not long in suspense, for at a given signal our artillery opened fire throwing their missiles of death right down the enemy's line and making the very earth tremble with the thunderstones, and following in quick succession, a cheer such as Southern soldiers only can give and a terrible crash of musketry told us that Longstreet and his gallant braves had succeeded in getting on the enemy's flank and was dealing out death and destruction to them in their usual style. But the enemy was too strong on that portion of the line to give way easily and fought for some time. But in half an hour from the commencement of the attack I saw the Yankees retreating, and our boys yelling like madmen in hot pursuit. The Yankees did not seem to be able to organize their shattered lines, and it was evident to all that if fresh troops were not on hand to check these flying fragments of regiments and brigades, the field would be ours.

But about this time I saw immediately in our front solid masses of fresh troops, moving up between us and the victory, and now our time for action had come. The time to try our manhood, the long looked for hour when we should meet the enemy on his own soil. I prayed God in that hour to assist me to do my whole duty to my country. The spirits of the troops were never better, and as Gen'l. Wilcox rode along down the line giving orders to charge, cheer after cheer filled the air almost drowning the sound of shells that were bursting above and around us. The proud banner which waved amid the wild tempest of battle at Williamsburg, Gaines Mills, Frazier's Farm, Sharpesburg, and Chancellorsville never rose more proudly than today. And as we moved forward in a perfect storm of shot, shell and canister, we felt that the starry cross must triumph.

Union Counterattack

In less than five minutes from the time, the Yankees were seen advancing, and death had commenced his work in good earnest. The battle now rages furiously, but our lines move onward—straight onward. The roaring of artillery,—grape and canister that came plunging through our ranks,—bullets thick as hailstones in winter, men falling on every side as leaves fall when shaken by the rude blasts of Autumn, is terrible, yet our men falter not, and we succeed in breaking their first and second lines of battle, capturing many prisoners, artillery, and colors. At the third and last line we met stern resistance; here for the third time since the war began we met the famous Irish Brigade, and they fought with a bravery worthy of a better cause. The troops on their immediate right and left gave way, leaving them exposed to an oblique fire from both flanks in addition to that from the front. Yet under the terrible fire they did not run, but retreated slowly and in good order, and returning our fire, but leaving the ground literally covered with their dead. They were, in fact, almost annihilated, and yet one regiment of them formed square around a piece of artillery and carried it some distance by hand, loading and firing it very rapidly, the square opening to allow them to fire, but at last they had to abandon it.

We drove them to the foot of the hill on which was posted their reserve artillery, but there meeting reenforcements and seeing our terribly thinned ranks they made another stand. Wilcox seeing the valor of his troops, moved among them and before them, as if courting death by his own daring intrepidity. The fight goes on, and the blood flows like water. But few are left unhurt, and with ranks now torn and bleeding, capture or annihilation inevitable if we remain longer, we all feel that something must be done, and that speedily. Some one gives the order to fall back, no one knows from where the order emanated. Some obey it, some do not. There were no longer companies or regiments, scarcely brigades, for Barksdale's had completely overlapped ours and we were mingled in glorious confusion. It was a line where every man seemed satisfied with any place and cared little for others, or what command he was fighting in. "Whiz" went a ball and burned the side of my head, just above the ear, cutting the hair nicely. The air was hot, and filled with sticks, rocks, dust and black smoke, almost suffocating, when I, with a few Mississippians, tried to make our way out back to where the line was trying to form.

After getting back about a hundred yards, we found that we had run into a gang of Yankees. For some unaccountable reason the troops on our left had not advanced and thereby had allowed the enemy to get into the rear. The first thing I knew there was a line of guns leveled on us, and one of the Yankees yelled out, "Surrender, you d—d gray backs." I saw at a glance that we were "gone up" and no help for it. In company with a large number of officers and men who had been captured in the same trap, I was hurried to the rear, feeling badly enough, and could have been bought for five cents. When I arrived in the rear of the lines, I found about fifty men and about a dozen officers from the old 9th. I was glad to see them, for misery loves company.

3
Pickett's Charge

Bruce Catton

The noted historian Bruce Catton is the author of *Grant Takes Command*, *A Stillness at Appomattox*, *Mr. Lincoln's Army*, and other books and articles on the Civil War. In this excerpt from *Gettysburg: The Final Fury*, Catton describes General George Pickett's charge into the center of the Union defenses on Cemetery Ridge on the third and final day of fighting at Gettysburg. About 14,000 Rebel soldiers marched across an open field into the teeth of Union cannon and rifle fire—a desperate attempt to break the Union defenses. The Confederates reached the Union line in only once place—at an angle in the line where the Rebels were repulsed after brief hand-to-hand fighting. Pickett's divisions eventually retreated, leaving almost half of their men behind. With a historian's eye for detail and a novelist's sense of narrative pace, Catton describes Pickett's fatal charge, the assault that lost the battle for General Robert E. Lee's army.

A long [General Winfield] Hancock's defensive line on the [Cemetery Ridge] Union soldiers looked to the woods that fringed the opposite ridge a mile to the west, and as the guns fell silent they could see a long ripple of movement, and men with rifles and flags stepped out into the open. The Federals saw, knew that the real test lay not far ahead, and muttered to one another:

"Here they are. Here comes the infantry."

Military men then had, and still have, a succinct expression: infantry is the Queen of Battles. Cavalry was very useful, and there were many jobs where powerful artillery was

Excerpted from *Gettysburg: The Final Fury*, by Bruce Catton (Garden City: Doubleday & Company, Inc., 1974). Copyright © 1974 by Bruce Catton. All rights reserved. Reprinted with permission of Doubleday & Company, Inc.

essential, but when the final showdown came the foot soldier carrying a rifle was the important figure. The big guns had done what they could; now it was the infantry that would settle matters.

The open hollow between the ridges was the great valley of the shadow of death, and when the smoke drifted up and spun away into misty fragments it was as if a curtain had gone up to reveal the stage of some terrible unimaginable theater. The Federal soldiers on the eastern ridge looked west; they were veterans and then had been in many battles, but what they saw now took their breath away. Some of them had seventy-five years yet to live and some of them had no more than ten minutes, but until they died they remembered the scene that now presented itself. There it was, for the last time in this war, perhaps for the last time anywhere, the fearful pageantry and color of war in the old style, beautiful and majestic and hideous; fighting men lined up in double and triple ranks, a solid mile from flank to flank, slashed red flags overhead, sunlight glinting off polished musket barrels—the flower of Lee's army coming forward, unhurried, for the great test that would determine whether there would hereafter be one nation or two between Canada and the Rio Grande . . . and whether Americans on American soil could continue to own other men and women, or be owned by them, as cattle and horses are owned.

Pickett's Men Move Forward

The flower of Lee's army: 15,000 men, or perhaps a slightly smaller number, coming along with Pickett's division as the spearhead. Out of the trees and the shadows they came, and when they reached the open they paused and dressed their lines with parade-ground formality, as if they proposed to go about this business of crushing the Yankee host with a flourish in high style, pride and courage blending into arrogance and dauntless confidence. The ranked Confederate cannon were all silent as the infantry passed through, and on Cemetery Ridge the Union guns also were silent, and it was as if both armies waited to savor the war's supreme moment of drama.

The advancing Confederates had nearly a mile to go, and the odds were against them. Tough General [James] Longstreet, who had urged Lee to swing off around the Union left to strike for the unprotected rear, did not think this attack could possibly succeed, and when Pickett rode up to him to say that the ranks were all formed and to ask if he should begin the charge, Longstreet was unable to put the order into words and could only bow his head in a choked gesture of command.

These men were going to march uphill to strike the Union line where it was strongest, and they would be a perfect target. Furthermore, if they themselves were the flower of Lee's army, the men they were about to fight were the flower of [General George] Meade's army—Hancock's II Corps, mostly, with unbroken elements from the shattered I Corps, and with the powerful VI Corps available for use if reinforcements were needed. After the war Longstreet said that he had warned Lee that "no fifteen thousand men ever arrayed for battle can take that position," and whether he actually said it or just thought afterward that he should have said it, his appraisal stands. The thing just could not be done.

But the way it was tried still commands attention.

The great charge actually began in silence, as if the two armies consciously willed a lull while the long lines were carefully dressed. The Confederate guns could not fire while the infantrymen were passing through their line, and most of the waiting Federal cannon had used their long-range ammunition in the earlier artillery duel and had to wait until the attackers came close; and the troops were not yet within effective musket range. So the long lines came forward, brimming up to the long diagonal of the Emmitsburg road, crossing it, and pausing once more to perfect the dress. Then they moved on again, and if the waiting Federals looked closely they could have seen a Confederate officer who held his sword high over his head, with his black felt hat on the lifted point of it as a guide for his brigade—Brigadier General Lewis Armistead, who was coming over the valley to meet death and an old friend [General Hancock]. . . .

Union Troops Open a Deadly Fire on Pickett's Men

When the Confederates formed their lines just before beginning to advance, they had designated a "little clump of trees" on Cemetery Ridge as their objective. It was a wholly unremarkable little grove, hardly big enough for a family to have a picnic in, and it had open fields all around it, with a low fence of stones and rails running along the western side.

It lay on the skyline as a good landmark, right in the center of Hancock's line. Here was the spot Pickett's men were to hit, and as the long lines swung across the Emmitsburg road the flanking elements began to move in toward the center so that the entire mass could strike the selected place with maximum impact.

But at about the time the Southerners crossed the road they began to have trouble. Much of Hancock's artillery might be out of action, waiting for close range, but when the attackers crossed the road they came within reach of the infantry's muskets, and these were the deadliest weapons of

On the final day of fighting, General Pickett led the fatal charge on Cemetery Ridge in a desperate attempt to break Union defenses.

all. The field guns were frightening and under certain circumstances they could be devastating, but in the long run, battles were decided by musket fire and so it was here. As Pickett's men advanced, the right wing of the charging column had to cross an open space beyond which there was a brigade of Vermont infantry, and this infantry moved forward a hundred yards or so, swung to its right, caught the end of the Confederate line in flank and opened a killing fire that shattered the flank and sent the survivors crowding off toward the center. At the same time a long rank of reserve artillery, posted to the south of Hancock's infantry, began to fire obliquely down the length of the Confederate ranks, adding to the carnage. The right end of the assaulting column was crippled before it got to close quarters.

At the northern end of the line there was a similar story. Some Ohio troops had worked their way forward, like the Vermonters farther south, and these caught the Confederate left flank with a shockingly effective fire. Along the low stone wall facing the Confederates on this part of the field were Union soldiers armed with smooth-bore muskets in place of the rifled pieces that were standard equipment; but the range now was so close that the smooth-bores (charged with buckshot, they were today, usually with an overload) could have full effect, and the Confederates were under terrible fire from two sides.

Then the Union artillery got into the action again. There were plenty of guns here, off a few hundred yards to the north of the little clump of trees, and if they had used up their long-range ammunition, they had plenty of canister, and now they got off a furious blast. (Canister was the gunners' close-range ammunition; a charge of canister consisted simply of a tin can full of lead slugs somewhat smaller than golf balls. When the gun was fired, the tin can disintegrated and the slugs went out in an expanding cloud, like a charge fired from a monstrously over-sized sawed-off shotgun. Within 200 yards this weapon was murderous beyond belief.) When these guns were fired, men who saw it all said that the advancing Confederates disappeared in a boiling cloud of dust and smoke, in which knapsacks and muskets and horrible fragments of human bodies were tossed high in the air; one Federal soldier remembered that there came from this part of the field a strange sound that was like an agonized gasp of pain coming from hundreds of throats. No one seems to have remembered hearing any cheers from either side. One soldier recalled only "a vast mournful roar" that seemed to rise from the entire field.

Thus, as the great charge drew near to its objective, both its flanks had been broken. (Flanking fire was especially deadly, because the line that was being flanked could not make any reply to it and was itself utterly vulnerable; fire that came slicing along the length of an infantry line simply could not miss, and no troops could stand it very long.) Longstreet, looking on from the rear, saw what was happening and remarked to a British observer who was standing beside him that the attack was going to fail.

Confederates Reach the Union Lines

But it had not failed yet, and if the flanks of the Confederate line crumbled, the center was strong. It built up its strength now, in front of the memorable clump of trees. (The trees are still there, protected by an iron fence, all set off with monuments and plaques.) As they came in close— whites-of-the-eyes range, at last—the Confederates halted. Standing, kneeling, or lying at full length, they opened their own rifle fire on the Federals. An infantry attack in the Civil War rarely involved an unbroken run forward followed by hand-to-hand work with the bayonet. The object usually was to try to build up an overpowering rifle fire at close range, gaining superior fire power at the point of contact. Even with their broken flanks, the Confederates were accomplishing this here, and along the low wall that marked the Union front just before and to the immediate right and left of the clump of trees there were more Confederates than Federals in action.

For the next few minutes this irregular rectangle of ground, a hundred yards deep by two or three hundred yards wide, was the bloody cockpit of the whole war, the place where men on foot with guns in their hands would arrive at a verdict. In this rectangle there was little work by the artillery. The Confederate guns to the west could not fire into this place without hitting their own men, and the Union guns here were out of action. A regular army battery of six guns commanded by Lieutenant Alonzo Cushing had been posted just north of the trees; by the time the Confederates came up to close range, five of the six guns had been put out of action, and when Cushing got off a final shot

from the one gun that remained, he was killed and most of
the gun crew went down with him. The climax of Pickett's
charge was an infantry fight pure and simple.

It was fought out with unremitting fury. Some of Pickett's men broke in across the stone wall and knelt amid
Cushing's idle guns to fire point-blank at the defending infantry. Some of the defenders found the fire too hot to bear
and withdrew; on a narrow front, and for the moment, Pickett's men had actually broken the Union line. If they could
widen the break and hold on to the ground gained until help
came, they would have the battle won. . . .

Nowadays a visitor can stand by the clump of trees and
see the whole battlefield, and it is hard to realize that hardly
anything was visible to the men who were doing the fighting. This battle was fought in a blinding fog—a choking,
reeking, impenetrable mist of powder smoke—smoke from
the cannon and from the infantry rifles—lying close to the
ground and drifting up toward the sky until some breeze
might carry it away. Directly to the west of the focal point of
the battle Lee himself watched and could see nothing—just
an occasional glimpse of tossing flags and stabbing flames
when the smoke would thin out temporarily. Longstreet ordered a brigade forward to reinforce Pickett, and the men
could not see their objective because of the smoke clouds;
they drifted far off to the right, came up against a waiting
rank of Federal cannon and the spirited Vermonters, and
were torn apart and compelled to retreat without having had
the slightest effect on the course of the battle. . . .

For a brief time the Confederates had the advantage,
but they could not hold it. Crowding in to lay fire on the
Federals in and on both sides of the fated little grove, they
had an advantage in numbers, but there were too many
Union soldiers in the immediate vicinity, and these were
called over on the double. They came in swarms, formal
military formation lost as they ran up to get into action at
close range. The crowd became so dense that some of these
reinforcements, halting to open fire on their enemies, hit
their own comrades in front of them—just as some of the
distant Confederate cannon, reaching out to hurt the Federals, struck down Confederates in the blind confusion.
From the crest of Cemetery Ridge, perhaps a hundred yards
behind the point of break-through, the Union regiments
that had retreated formed ranks anew, regained their nerve,

and opened a sharp counterattack. General Hancock, riding up to see that the front was restored, was shot from his horse with a wound that would keep him out of action until the following spring. General Gibbon also was shot down, severely wounded; but the Federal line stiffened and held without further direction, because in the end this was the private soldier's fight.

On the Confederate side it was Armistead who had led the contingent that broke the Federal line. He was still waving his sword, his black felt hat that had been on the point of the sword had slipped all the way down to the hilt; he laid his hand on one of dead Cushing's guns, urged his men on, a great figure of defiance—and then he fell with a mortal wound. An hour later, when Federal stretcher bearers were combing the littered field, he was still alive—enough so that he could stammer out a last message to his old friend Hancock. Then he died, while wounded Hancock was being carried from the field. The paths of these two men, which had parted in California more than two years earlier, had crossed again, for the last time.

The Confederates Retreat

Then, suddenly, as the men from the North and the men from the South struggled in the dense battle smoke, the climax was passed. The Confederate wave had reached highwater mark and it began to ebb; watching from his post on the western ridge, Lee could see the human debris of a broken charge drifting back down the long slope. Military formations had been broken, but for the most part the men were going back sullenly, not panicky fugitives but soldiers ready to turn and fight if the Federals attempted a pursuit. The Federals made no attempt. They had beaten back the supreme effort Lee's army could make, but they had just about exhausted themselves doing it. They were content to see their enemies go away.

From his headquarters behind the lines Meade rode forward, saw the littered field, and learned that his soldiers had won a great victory. He took off his hat, apparently preparing to give a great shout, then thought better of it and said, reverently, "Thank God!" A mile away Lee rode forward to rally the men who had made the charge, telling them simply: "It is all my fault."

That night, after dark, Lee issued instructions for the

organization of a wagon train to carry some of the thousands of wounded men back to Virginia. To an officer who received the orders, Lee said that he had never seen anything finer than the charge Pickett's men had made. If it had been supported properly, he said, it would have succeeded. Then his emotions broke through, and he cried aloud: "Oh, too bad! Too bad!"

4

The Wounded and Dead of Gettysburg

Kent Gramm

Kent Gramm, a contemporary novelist, is the author of *Gettysburg: A Meditation on War and Values*. In this text, whose chapter titles are patterned on those of Henry David Thoreau's *Walden*, Gramm reflects on the landscape of Gettysburg, Pennsylvania, which he visited frequently over a period of ten years. As Thoreau, in the mid-nineteenth century, ruminated on the natural landscape of Walden Pond, Gramm, in the late-twentieth century, ponders the landscape of the Gettysburg battlefield, imagining the great battle that took place there in the summer of 1863. In this passage from *Gettysburg*, Gramm places the contemporary reader in Gettysburg two or three days after the battle. Gramm's focus in this excerpt is the dead and wounded left behind at the battlefield after the fighting had ended.

Suppose you knew nothing of the battle and found yourself on the field July 5 or 6. What had happened? Your first effort would not be to look around and solve the puzzle, but to get out of there.

After the Great Battle

Before the visual horrors registered, you might be overcome physically. The smell fills your head and becomes a slippery growth in your stomach. One veteran wrote of throwing himself face to the ground and vomiting himself empty. Many were made quite ill by the odor alone.

Excerpted from *Gettysburg: A Meditation on War and Values*, by Kent Gramm (Bloomington: Indiana University Press, 1994). Copyright © 1994 by Kent Gramm. Reprinted with permission.

Before the stretcher-bearers and ambulances finished their work picking up the perhaps ten thousand wounded actually lying on the field, you would have heard the constant moans and screams, the unceasing pleas for water whispered, sobbed, screamed, begged—a nightmarish and pathetic cacophony everywhere rising across the fields and at your feet. You would have seen men with every conceivable bullet and artillery wound, mouths bubbling blood, shot lungs and throats foaming and whistling, blood-soaked shattered limbs.

And the dead. In all positions—some restful, some in frozen, open-eyed terror or rage, some twisted with agony. In some of the fields you could have walked in any direction just stepping on the mutilated dead. Hundreds of Southerners were buried on the Rose Farm. The dead were bloated, sometimes moving before your eyes as gasses inside them shifted. Their faces were blackened by the hot sun; perhaps their fishlike mouths were ringed with gunpowder from the cartridges they had bitten open before being stricken. Their eyes bulged. Some seemed twice the size they should be.

That was not all: the dead were dismembered, lacerated, some naked in their death agonies having torn off their clothing, some shoeless and with pockets and haversacks turned inside-out, some with sides or abdomens shot away and organs spilled and rotten, crawling with maggots. (Green bottle flies were everywhere in the millions, covering dead and living.) Visitors reported hands and arms in tree limbs, boots lying with feet and legs still in them, heads on the fields and among the rocks: artillery was hideous in its effects. One female nurse described the headless trunk of a man sitting against a tree, arms shot off, the torn clothing of the drained body flapping in the breeze. Shell concussions flattened bodies against rocks, into shapeless horrors. All these were you and me, hit by bullets (21 inches of human body mass was needed to stop a bullet at 150 yards, a doctor calculated), by iron shell fragments, by solid shot. Clubbed muskets and bayonets. Heat, thirst, delirium. After a few days, buzzards.

Makeshift Field Hospitals

Hospitals everywhere behind the battle lines and in town: farmhouses, barns, public buildings, schools, churches,

After the fighting had ended, the landscape of Gettysburg was a night-marish scene littered with the broken bodies of wounded and dead soldiers.

stores, houses. Some of these buildings still have bloodstains on the floors. Hundreds lay on boards placed over pews in churches; men were put on floors, tables; they covered all the space in Gettysburg side by side, with only a few nurses and doctors for every several hundred wounded. A woman who nursed Confederates at the main building of Pennsylvania College said that each morning a dozen or more corpses lay outside the door for burial.

Doctors operated and sawed, sleeves rolled up, covered all over with blood, hundreds of men waiting for each of them. Some stood for thirty-six hours at a tune, held up like Moses by others; at least one doctor became hysterical. There was little support staff, no understanding of germ theory, and the big, soft Minié bullet smashed bones, leaving nothing much to reconstruct: outside windows of temporary hospitals and piled in front of the big tents lay arms, hands, legs, feet. Union doctors had chloroform and ether;

when Southern doctors ran short they resorted to "Confederate chloroform"—whisky. Men lay for hours, then days, on hard floors and balconies, with little or no straw under them, as long as six days without food—waiting for such treatment as could be given.

Burying the Dead of Gettysburg

Back on the fields burial groups, some men with handkerchiefs tied uselessly across their faces, dug graves and marked them for the Union casualties. Soldiers talked loudly—deafened by two or three days of battle—doing the horrifying, disgusting, sad, numbing work. Lee's dead men had no one but the Yankees to bury them. (That is why most of the photographed dead at Gettysburg are Southern—their bodies were still there when the photographers arrived.) Several days after Lee retreated, the remaining bodies were turned into shallow trenches, dirt hastily shoveled back over them. Visitors reported that hands, feet, even faces protruded from the soil—and that at night the decomposing bodies so near the surface gave a phosphorescent glow across the ground.

Southern prisoners were ordered to help with burials, but the work was done in revulsive haste. Sometimes penciled lettering on a shingle or piece of bark said "54 Rebs."; sometimes someone would write a name and company on a board half-buried or on a cartridge-box flap. But in a short time all such markings would be gone. There are probably still Southern bodies in the Valley of Death and elsewhere at Gettysburg. Gregory Coco reports findings of bones as recently as 1977, and figures that a thousand Confederate graves still remain undiscovered in Adams County.

The Debris of Battle

The fields were covered with ramrods, rifles, bayonets, clothing, and every item a soldier might have carried: toothbrushes, Bibles, books, photographs, cards, letters, paper, pens. The trees were pocked with bullets; during the next thirty years many trees in McPherson's Woods died from lead poisoning.

Dead horses lay everywhere, about five thousand. Crops were trampled, fruit trees were shattered, fences had been torn apart and burned, barns were partly disassembled; carpets, walls, mattresses, blankets, sofas, tables, yards, and parcels of earth everywhere were soaked with human blood.

In the Northern states, and in towns and villages of the South, people stood and read the lists.

At the end of anger are grief, horror, revulsion, pity. As you stand in the dizzying stench and gasp your disbelief, you wonder what these creatures fought for. Were the issues as important as whatever set the red ants on the black in *Walden*, and had there been heroics? What was it all for? The aftermath of battle, and the fighting itself, are clean divorced from the causes of the war; things went on under their own power. It could have been Oates attacked on Seminary Ridge by Cutler's Brigade as easily as the Alabamians charging Little Round Top. "O my people, they which lead thee cause thee to err!" What is all this waste and guilt, this sorrow and despair, the suffering and ghastly death—*for?* What is the meaning of the battle?

Chapter 2

Why the South Lost at Gettysburg

1

General Longstreet Blames General Lee for the South's Defeat

James Longstreet

After the death of General Thomas (Stonewall) Jackson at the Battle of Chancellorsville in May 1863, General James Longstreet became General Robert E. Lee's most trusted general. Lee once referred to Longstreet as "my old warhorse." At Gettysburg, however, Longstreet strongly opposed Lee's battle tactics. Lee wanted to attack the Union army, while Longstreet preferred to fight on the defensive, coaxing Union General George Meade to initiate combat. Lee sent Longstreet's corps to smash the Union southern flank on the second day of fighting at Gettysburg, an unsuccessful attack that cost the Confederates thousands of men. Longstreet was somewhat tardy in getting his troops into action for that engagement, leading some military historians to blame Longstreet for the South's defeat at Gettysburg. Longstreet also opposed Lee's decision to attack the Union center on the third day of combat, the assault that ultimately lost the battle for Lee. Thirty years after the war, Longstreet published *From Manassas to Appomattox: Memoirs of the Civil War in America*, in which he defended his own actions at Gettysburg and, in doing so, pinned the blame for the South's defeat on Lee.

It should be stated that kindest relations were maintained between General Lee and myself until interrupted by politics in 1867.

Excerpted from "Gettysburg—Third Day," by James Longstreet, in *From Manassas to Appomattox: Memoirs of the Civil War in America*, edited by James I. Robertson Jr. (Bloomington: Indiana University Press, 1960). Copyright © 1960 by Indiana University Press.

It is difficult to reconcile these facts with the reports put out after his death by members of his family and of his staff; and *post-bellum* champions, that indicate his later efforts to find points by which to so work up public opinion as to shift the disaster [at Gettysburg] to my shoulders.

Some of the statements of the members of the staff have been referred to. General Fitzhugh Lee claims evidence that General Lee said that he would have gained the battle if he had had General [Thomas (Stonewall)] Jackson with him. But he had Jackson in the Sharpsburg campaign, which was more blundering than that of Gettysburg. In another account Fitzhugh Lee wrote of General Lee,—

"He told the father of the writer, his brother, that he was controlled too far by the great confidence he felt in the fighting qualities of his people, and by assurances of most of his higher officers."

No assurances were made from officers of the First Corps, but rather objections. The only assurances that have come to light, to be identified, are those of General [Jubal] Early, who advised the battle, but *from the other end of the line from his command*, which should have given warning that it did not come from the heart of a true soldier.

Attacks Against Superior Forces

And this is the epitome of the Confederate battle. The army when it set out on the campaign was all that could be desired, (except that the arms were not all of the most approved pattern), but it was despoiled of two of its finest brigades, Jenkins's and Corse's of Pickett's division, and was fought out by detail. The greatest number engaged at any one time was on the first day, when twenty-six thousand engaged twenty thousand of the First and part of the Eleventh Corps. On the afternoon of the second day about seventeen thousand were engaged on the right, and at night about seven thousand on the left; then later at night about three thousand near the centre. On the third day about twelve thousand were engaged at daylight and until near noon, and in the afternoon fifteen thousand,—all of the work of the second and third days against an army of seventy thousand and more of veteran troops in strong position defended by field-works.

General Lee was on the field from about three o'clock of the afternoon of the first day. Every order given the

General Longstreet maintained that lack of information and support from Lee were the direct causes of his unsuccessful attack of the Union southern flank.

troops of the First Corps on that field up to its march on the forenoon of the 2d was issued in his presence. If the movements were not satisfactory in time and speed of moving, it was his power, duty, and privilege to apply the remedy, but it was not a part of a commander's duty or privilege to witness things that did not suit him, fail to apply the remedy, and go off and grumble with his staff-officers about it. In their efforts to show culpable delay in the movements of the First Corps on the 2d, some of the Virginia writers endeavor to show that General Lee did not even give me a guide to lead the way to the field from which his battle was to be opened. He certainly failed to go and look at it, and assist in selecting the ground and preparing for action.

Fitzhugh Lee says of the second day, "Longstreet was attacking the Marye's Hill of the position." At [the Battle of] Fredericksburg, General Burnside attacked at Marye's Hill in six or more successive assaults with some twenty or thirty thousand against three brigades under McLaws and Ransom and the artillery; he had about four hundred yards to march from his covered ways about Fredericksburg to Marye's Hill. When his last attack was repulsed in the evening, he arranged and gave his orders for the attack to be renewed in the morning, giving notice that he would lead it with the Ninth Corps, but, upon reports of his officers abandoned it. General Lee's assaulting columns of fifteen or twenty thousand had a march of a mile to attack double their numbers, better defended than were the three brigades of Confederates at Marye's Hill that drove back Burnside. The enemy on Cemetery Hill was in stronger position than the Confederates at Marye's Hill. . . .

Forty thousand men, unsupported as we were, could not have carried the position at Gettysburg. The enemy was there. Officers and men knew their advantage, and were resolved to stay until the hills came down over them. It is simply out of the question for a lesser force to march over broad, open fields and carry a fortified front occupied by a greater force of seasoned troops. . . .

Fitzhugh Lee quotes evidence of Governor Carroll, of Maryland, that General Lee said, "Longstreet is the hardest man to move in my army."

It does not look like generalship to lose a battle and a cause and then lay the responsibility upon others. He held command and was supported by his government. If his army did not suit him, his word could have changed it in a minute. If he failed to apply the remedy, it was his fault. Some claim that his only fault as a general was his tender, generous heart. But a heart in the right place looks more to the cause intrusted to its care than for hidden ways by which to shift its responsibility to the shoulders of those whose lives hang upon his word. . . .

At the Second Manassas my command relieved the pressure against Jackson. He called on me for relief by a route that would have taken an hour or an hour and a half. A way was found by which he was relieved in about thirty minutes. When relieved, he left the battle on my hands. I was at Sharpsburg all day; Jackson only about two and a half hours. At Fredericksburg, anticipating the move against him, half of my command was ordered to swing off from my right and join in his battle.

Longstreet Refutes the Charge
That He Delayed at Gettysburg

But General Lee's assertion seems to refer to the operations at Gettysburg, after Jackson had found his Happy Home. Let us see how far this assertion is supported by events. General Lee reported,—

"The advance of the enemy to the latter place (Gettysburg) was unknown, and, the weather being inclement, the march was conducted with a view to the comfort of the troops."

When, on the forenoon of the 2d, he decided upon his plan, the Second Corps was deployed in the immediate front of the enemy's line on our left, except two brigades sent off by General Early. One division of the Third was close on the right of the Second, all within thirty minutes' march of the enemy's lines. Two divisions of the Third Corps and two of the First were on Seminary Ridge. When the order was announced the divisions on Seminary Ridge had to find their positions and deploy to the right. By the route ordered for the march it was five or six miles to the point at which the battle was to be opened. The troops of the Third had a shorter route. The march of the First was made in time for prompt deployment on the right of the Third.

We were left to our own resources in finding ground upon which to organize for battle. The enemy had changed position somewhat after the march was ordered, but as we were not informed of his position before the march, we could not know of the change. The Confederate commander did not care to ride near us, to give information of a change, to assist in preparing for attack, nor to inquire if new and better combinations might be made.

Four brigades of the right of the Third Corps were assigned as part of my command. The engagement was to be general. My artillery combat was opened at three P.M., followed in half an hour by the infantry, and I made progressive battle until sundown. A division of the Second Corps attacked on our left at nightfall, and later two brigades.

Other parts of the Second and Third Corps did not move to the battle.

On the 3d I was ordered to organize the column of assault, the other corps to co-operate and assist the battle. There was an affair on the Confederate left before the assaulting columns were organized, brought on by attack of the enemy. The assaulting force marched at one P.M. Its work has been described, but it is important to note that neither of the other corps took part in the battle while the Southern chief stood in view of the attack and near the rear of those corps. So it looks as if the commander of the First Corps was easier to move than any one in his army, rather than harder, and his chief left him to fight the battles alone.

After the retreat, and when resting on the south banks of the Rapidan, reading of the progress of the march of General Rosecrans's army towards Georgia, it seemed sinful to lie there idle while our comrades in the West were so in need of assistance, and I wrote the Secretary of War suggesting that a detachment should be sent West from the idle army. General Lee objected, but the suggestion was ordered to be executed. In this instance the subordinate was easier to move than his chief, though the interests of the cause depended largely on the movement of the latter.

2

General Gordon Exonerates General Lee for the South's Defeat

John B. Gordon

General John B. Gordon, a Georgia attorney and lifelong defender of slavery, fought with General Robert E. Lee in most of the major engagements in the Virginia theater during the Civil War—Manassas, Antietam, Seven Pines, Chancellorsville, Gettysburg, the Wilderness, Petersburg—and was present at Lee's surrender at Appomattox. After the war, in 1903, Gordon published *Reminiscences of the Civil War*, throughout which he expressed his great admiration for Lee and praise for Lee's military strategies. In this passage from that text, Gordon absolves Lee of the Confederate defeat at Gettysburg, placing the blame instead on Lee's subordinates for "a lack of cheerful, prompt, and intelligent cooperation" and "delays that General Lee could not foresee nor provide against."

It is a great loss to history and to posterity that General Lee did not write his own recollections as General Grant did. It was his fixed purpose to do so for some years after the war ended. From correspondence and personal interviews with him, I know that he was profoundly impressed with the belief that it was his duty to write, and he expended much time and labor in getting the material for such a work. From his reports, which are models of official papers, were necessarily excluded the free and full comments upon plans, movements, men, failures, and the reasons for such failures, as

Excerpted from *Reminiscences of the Civil War*, by John B. Gordon (New York: Charles Scribner's Sons, 1903).

they appeared to him, and of which he was the most competent witness. To those who knew General Lee well, and who added to this knowledge a just appreciation of his generous nature, the assumption by him of entire responsibility for the failure at Gettysburg means nothing except an additional and overwhelming proof of his almost marvellous magnanimity. He was commander-in-chief, and as such and in that sense he was responsible; but in that sense he was also responsible for every act of every officer and every soldier in his army. This, however, is not the kind of responsibility under discussion. This is not the standard which history will erect and by which he will be judged. If by reason of repeated mistakes or blunders he had lost the confidence and respect of his army, and for this cause could no longer command its cordial and enthusiastic support, this fact would fix his responsibility for the failure. But no such conditions appertained. As already stated, the confidence in him before and after the battle was boundless. Napoleon Bonaparte never more firmly held the faith of Frenchmen, when thrones were trembling before him, than did Lee hold the faith of his devoted followers, amidst the gloom of his heaviest disasters.

Lee's Plan at Gettysburg Promised Success

If his plan of battle was faulty, then for this he is responsible; but if his general plan promised success, and if there was a lack of cheerful, prompt, and intelligent cooperation in its execution, or if there were delays that General Lee could not foresee nor provide against, and which delays or lack of cooperation enabled [Union] General [George] Meade to concentrate his reserves behind the point of contemplated attack, then the responsibility is shifted to other shoulders.

There was nothing new or especially remarkable in General Lee's plans. Novelties in warfare are confined rather to its implements than to the methods of delivering battle. To Hannibal and Cæsar, to Frederick and Napoleon, to Grant and Lee, to all great soldiers, the plan was familiar. It was to assault along the entire line and hold the enemy to hard work on the wings, while the artillery and heaviest impact of infantry penetrated the left centre. Cooperation by every part of his army was expected and essential. However well trained and strong may be the individual horses in a team, they will never move the stalled wagon when one pulls forward while the other holds back. They must all pull together, or the heavily loaded wagon will never be carried to the top of the hill. Such cooperation at Gettysburg was only partial, and limited to comparatively small forces. Pressure—hard, general, and constant pressure—upon Meade's right would have called him to its defence and weakened his centre. That pressure was only spasmodic and of short duration. Lee and his plan could only promise success on the proviso that the movement was both general and prompt. It was neither. Moments in battle are pregnant with the fate of armies. When the opportune moment to strike arrives, the blow must fall; for the next instant it may be futile. Not only moments, but hours, of delay occurred. I am criticising officers for the lack of complete cooperation, not for unavoidable delays. I am simply stating facts which must necessarily affect the verdict of history. Had all the commands designated by General Lee cooperated by a simultaneous assault, thus preventing Meade from grouping his troops around his centre, and had the onset upon that centre occurred in the early morning, as intended by Lee, it requires no partiality to see that this great commander's object would have been assuredly achieved. That the plan involved hazard is undoubtedly true. All battles between such troops as confronted each other at Gettysburg are hazardous and uncertain. If the commanders of the Confederate and Union armies had waited for opportunities free of hazard and uncertainty, no great battle would have 'been fought and the war never would have ended. The question which history will ask is this: Was General Lee justified in expecting success? The answer will be that, with his experience in meeting the same Union army at Fredericksburg, at the second Manassas, in the seven-days' battles around Richmond, and at Chancellorsville; with an army behind him which he believed well-nigh invincible, and which army believed its commander well-nigh infallible; with a victory for his troops on the first day at Gettysburg, the completeness of which had been spoiled only by an untimely and fatal halt; with the second day's battle ending with alternate successes and indecisive results; and with the expectation of prompt action and vigorous united cooperation, he was abundantly justified in confidently expecting success.

[British General] Wellington at Waterloo and Meade at Gettysburg, each held the highlands against his antagonist. Wellington on Mont-Saint-Jean, and Meade on Cemetery

Ridge, had the bird's-eye view of the forces of attack. The English batteries on the plateau and the Union batteries on Cemetery Heights commanded alike the intervening undulations across which the charging columns must advance. Behind Mont-Saint-Jean, to conceal Wellington's movements from Napoleon's eye, were the woodlands of Soignies. Behind Cemetery Ridge, to conceal Meade's movements from the field-glasses of Lee, was a sharp declivity, a protecting and helpful depression. As the French under Napoleon at Waterloo, so the Confederates under Lee at Gettysburg, held the weaker position. In both cases the assailants sought to expel their opponents from the stronger lines. I might add another resemblance in the results which followed. Waterloo decreed the destiny of France, of England, of Europe. Gettysburg, not so directly or immediately, but practically, decided the fate of the Confederacy.

There were points of vast divergence. The armies which met at Waterloo were practically equal. This was not true of the armies that met at Gettysburg. Napoleon's artillery far exceeded that of Wellington. Lee's was far inferior to Meade's, in the metal from which the guns were moulded, as well as in number. Waterloo was a rout, Gettysburg a repulse. Napoleon, in the ensuing panic, was a deserted fugitive. Lee rode amidst his broken lines calmly majestic, the idol of his followers. With no trace of sympathy for Napoleon's selfish aims, with righteous condemnation of his vaulting ambition, one cannot fail to realize the profound pathos of his position on that dismal night of wildest panic and lonely flight. Abandoned by fortune, deserted by his army, discrowned and doomed, he is described by [Victor] Hugo as having not an organized company to comfort him, not even his faithful Old Guard to rally around him. In Lee's army there was neither panic nor precipitate retreat. There was no desertion of the great commander. Around him still stood his heroic legions, with confidence in him unshaken, love for him unabated, ready to follow his lead and to fight under his orders to the last extremity.

3

Lee's Command Methods Ensured Failure

Michael A. Palmer

Michael A. Palmer, a professor of history at East Carolina University, is the author of *Lee Moves North: Robert E. Lee on the Offensive*. In this text, published in 1998, Palmer sharply criticizes General Robert E. Lee's command methods and battle strategy during the Battle of Gettysburg. According to Palmer, Lee's "decentralized approach to command and control" spelled doom for the Army of Northern Virginia at Gettysburg. Palmer accuses Lee of giving indirect orders, of failing to formulate an overall plan of action for the battle, and of ordering a "senseless, even suicidal assault" on the third and final day of combat. In Palmer's view, the South lost at Gettysburg because of General Robert E. Lee.

What is also clear is that Lee's command methods all but ensured failure on the afternoon of the first day at Gettysburg. The decentralized approach to command and control that served Lee so well on other occasions failed him on July 1 because the two elements necessary to make the system work—competent subordinates, and clearly defined and enunciated plans and objectives—were lacking. [General Richard] Ewell, as Lee had feared and should have known after Winchester, was no Stonewall Jackson. Despite the fact that Lee had ordered the army to concentrate around Gettysburg, Ewell was clearly confused about whether or not Lee wished to actually fight a battle there. What Lee needed to do late in the afternoon of July 1 was

Excerpted from *Lee Moves North: Robert E. Lee on the Offensive*, by Michael A. Palmer (New York: John Wiley & Sons, Inc., 1998). Copyright © 1998 by Michael A. Palmer. Reprinted by permission.

to take command of his own army. Lee was a West Pointer, a trained engineering officer. He could see the high ground south of the town and appreciate its importance. All he needed to do was to direct—to order—both Ewell and [General A.P.] Hill to advance. Instead, Lee asked Hill if he could attack; Hill, tired and sick, declined. Lee's orders to Ewell, as they are reflected in the commanding general's report, were cautionary in the extreme and hardly direct.

Why did Lee fail to issue the necessary orders? The reasons are two: first, to issue such direct orders would, of course, have been out of character; and second, on the afternoon of July 1, Lee himself did not know whether or not he wished to bring on a general engagement. Not until the evening did he finally decide to continue the battle. As he reasoned in his preliminary report:

It had not been intended to fight a general battle at such a distance from our base, unless attacked by the enemy, but, finding ourselves unexpectedly confronted by the Federal Army, it became a matter of difficulty to withdraw through the mountains with our large trains. At the same time, the country was unfavorable for collecting supplies while in the presence of the enemy's main body, as he was enabled to restrain our foraging parties by occupying the passes of the mountains with regular and local troops. A battle thus became, in a measure, unavoidable. Encouraged by the successful issue of the engagement of the first day, and in view of the valuable results that would ensue from the defeat of the army of General Meade, it was thought advisable to renew the attack.

Lee, in his late afternoon effort to pass the responsibility for continuing the battle to Ewell and Hill, was avoiding his own accountability as commander.

Lack of a Battle Plan

Lee, having finally decided to fight his "general engagement," needed, as soon as possible—preferably before dawn—to formulate a plan of action for the coming day. This he failed to do, in part because of his uncertainty about the enemy's positions, but also because of a lack of cooperation on the part of his corps commanders. Ewell and his division commanders were reluctant to yield the ground they had won and to move during the night from their lines east of Gettysburg to new positions south and west of the town on Hill's immediate left. Lee's unwillingness to order Ewell to move ensured that it would be extremely difficult for the commanding general to coordinate the movements of Ewell, on the far left, and [General James] Longstreet, who was coming up on the far right. Nor was Longstreet particularly cooperative. Lee wanted the First Corps to attack on the right, but Longstreet, who believed that it was a mistake to assume the tactical offensive, objected. He proposed instead that the entire army maneuver around the Federal left flank. Lee insisted; meanwhile, more time slipped away, and with it went the opportunity for the generals to rest before the coming action. Lee rode off, leaving Longstreet angered and disappointed.

It was midmorning before Lee had finalized his plan. Longstreet would launch the main attack with two divisions—those of Major Generals Lafayette McLaws and John Bell Hood—against the Federal left and roll up [Union General George] Meade's flank. Ewell would launch his attack in support and, if practicable, seize the hills before him. Lee set no deadlines; both attacks would commence when the respective commanders believed the troops were ready.

Unfortunately, Ewell grew tired of waiting for Longstreet. He attacked on his own and, worse yet, proved himself incapable of coordinating the actions of his three divisions. Each struck the Federals in turn, and to little effect. Lee later told William Allan that Ewell could not "act with decision" and that as a result, [General Robert] Rodes, [General Jubal] Early, and [General Edward] Johnson "attacked and were hurt in detail."

Longstreet's Delay

Nevertheless, Lee had not expected much from Ewell's attack; the main assault was to come on the Confederate right flank. But as the hours passed, and Longstreet's attack failed to materialize, Lee became increasingly agitated. In his reports on the battle, he made no mention of any delay on Longstreet's part, but memoirists, especially those who served on Lee's staff, accused the First Corps commander of an unnecessary delay that may have cost the Confederacy the battle—and to some minds, the war. Longstreet, in his own memoirs, claimed that he moved as promptly as possible and blamed the delay on Lee's failure to issue his orders more promptly. But G. Moxley Sorrel, the First Corps chief of staff, accused Longstreet of "apathy" in his preparation for the attack, rooted in his dislike for Lee's plan. Jeffry D. Wert, whose biography of Longstreet provides an excellent reconstruction of the timeline of Lee's decisions, concluded that Longstreet "deserves censure for the performance on the morning of July 2. He allowed his disagreement with Lee's decision to affect his conduct."

Lee's Failure to Take Charge

But while Ewell's incompetence and Longstreet's recalcitrance were important factors, Lee's unwillingness to issue direct orders or to take charge of the battle lay at the root of the problem. He left the timing of the First Corps attack up to Longstreet, who saw fit to delay until 4:00 P.M. By then more Federal troops were in position, and there were too few hours remaining in the day to exploit fully a marked success, had one been gained. As on the first day of the battle, Lee's style of command and lack of direction ensured that his subordinates failed to make the most of the opportunities that lay before the Army of Northern Virginia.

Pickett's Suicidal Charge

It was not until the third day of the battle that Lee actually took charge, although by then the prospects of victory were few. The entire Federal army was now in position, dug in along a series of ridges and hills. Given the situation, the most sensible courses of action for Lee would have been to withdraw or to go over to the defensive and hope that the enemy would attack, a tactically sensible but logistically difficult option. Lee, of course, chose a third option: to assault the center of the Federal line—the infamous "Pickett's Charge."

No one can ever say with certainty why Lee ordered what, in retrospect, appears to have been a senseless, even suicidal assault. But consider Lee's determination to attack as but the last of a series of decisions stretching back to early April 1863. Recall the promises that Lee had made to [President Jefferson] Davis, [Secretary of War James] Seddon, and the cabinet about the supposed benefits of a Northern invasion. Do not overlook the incredible burdens that Lee had placed on his own shoulders and those of his men—not just to perform well, not simply to harass the Yankees, not solely to save Richmond for another campaigning season, but also to redress the imbalance of forces in the western theater, and, perhaps, even to win the war. How could Lee, his army as yet undefeated, possibly recross the Potomac River and return to Virginia empty-handed without having struck one final blow? Just as a worried Lee had felt compelled to cross the river a week earlier, he now felt compelled to stake all on a forlorn hope. When Pickett's Charge failed, Lee knew that he had lost more than a few thousand men, more than a battle, even more than his own campaign. As the survivors, battered and beaten, made their way back toward their lines, Lee spoke the truth when he lamented: "It is all my fault."

4

Lee Cannot Be Blamed for the South's Defeat

Douglas Southall Freeman

In 1935, Douglas Southall Freeman, the editor of the Richmond, Virginia, *News-Leader*, won a Pulitzer Prize for his exhaustive four-volume biography of Robert E. Lee. In Volume III of that work, Freeman considers the most controversial event of Lee's military career, the Battle of Gettysburg. In a chapter titled "Why Was Gettysburg Lost?" Freeman calls the Gettysburg campaign "a daring move" that was both politically and militarily justified. Freeman offers several reasons for the South's failure at Gettysburg, including mistakes by Lee's subordinates and a lack of coordination during assaults by Confederate troops. Ultimately, Freeman blames the South's defeat at Gettysburg on the reorganization of the Army of Northern Virginia forced upon Lee by the death of General Thomas (Stonewall) Jackson two months before Gettysburg at the Battle of Chancellorsville. In Freeman's view, Lee's reorganized army failed to respond with the precision necessary to carry the day at Gettysburg.

Despite Lee's example and influence, criticism of the Confederate operations at Gettysburg was not silenced in 1863 and has been expressed at intervals ever since. Where confined to the actual military details of the campaign, this criticism is easily analyzed, for no other American battle has been so fully studied, and concerning none is there more general agreement on the specific reasons for the failure of the losing army.

Excerpted from *R.E. Lee: A Biography*, vol. III, by Douglas Southall Freeman (New York: Charles Scribner's Sons, 1935). Renewal copyright © 1963 by Inez Goddin Freeman. Reprinted with permission.

The invasion itself was, of course, a daring move, but, in the circumstances that Lee faced, politically and in a military sense, it probably was justified. The first mistake was in connection with [General J.E.B.] Stuart's operations. To recapitulate this point, Lee intended to allow his cavalry commander latitude as to where he should enter Maryland. He is not to be blamed for giving Stuart discretion, nor is Stuart justly subject to censure for exercising it. But the *Beau Sabreur* of the South, by pushing on after he had encountered resistance east of the Bull Run Mountains, violated orders and deprived Lee of his services when most needed. He should have turned back then, as Lee had directed him to do should he find his advance hindered by the Federal columns. Stuart erred, likewise, in taking with him all the cavalry brigades that had been accustomed to doing the reconnaissance work of the Army of Northern Virginia. General Lee, for his part, was at fault in handling the cavalry left at his disposal. He overestimated the fighting value of [General Micah] Jenkins's and of [General John] Imboden's brigades, which had little previous experience except in raids, and he failed to keep in close touch with [General J.B.] Robertson and [General Samuel] Jones, who remained behind in Virginia. Once in Pennsylvania, Lee's operations were handicapped not only because he lacked sufficient cavalry, but also because he did not have Stuart at hand. He had become dependent upon that officer for information of the enemy's position and plans and, in Stuart's absence, he had no satisfactory form of military intelligence. It is not enough to say with General [Jubal] Early, in exculpation of Stuart, that Lee found the enemy in spite of the absence of his cavalry. Had "Jeb" Stuart been at hand, Lee would have had early information of the advance of the Federals and either would have outfooted them to Gettysburg or would have known enough about their great strength to refrain from attacking as he did. The injudicious employment of the Confederate horse during the Gettysburg campaign was responsible for most of the other mistakes on the Southern side and must always remain a warning of the danger of permitting the cavalry to lose contact with an army when the enemy's positions are unknown. In its consequences, the blunder was more serious than that which Hooker made at Chancellorsville in sending Stoneman on a raid when he should have had his mounted forces in front and on the flank of the XI Corps.

Tentative Commanders
and Thinly Spread Troops

The second reason for the Confederate defeat manifestly was the failure of [General Richard] Ewell to take Cemetery Hill when Lee suggested, after the Federal defeat on the afternoon of July 1, that he attack it. Had Ewell thrown Early forward, without waiting for [General Edward] Johnson, he probably could have taken the hill at any time prior to 4 P.M. or perhaps to 4:30. Ewell hesitated because he was unfamiliar with Lee's methods and had been trained in a different school of command. [General "Stonewall"] Jackson, who had always directed Ewell's operations, had been uniformly explicit in his orders and had never allowed discretion unless compelled to do so; Lee always trusted the tactical judgment of his principal subordinates unless he had to be peremptory. Ewell, moreover, was of a temperament to take counsel, and was puzzled and embarrassed when told to capture Cemetery Hill "if practicable." Lee could not be expected to change his system for Ewell, nor could Ewell be expected to change his nature after only two months under Lee.

The third reason for defeat was the extent of the Confederate line and the resultant thinness. Lee's front on the second day, from [General John B.] Hood's right, opposite Round Top, to the left of Johnson, was slightly more than five miles in length. Communication between the flanks was slow and difficult. Co-ordination of attack was almost impossible with a limited staff. Lee should have held to the decision reached late on the afternoon of the 1st and considered again on the morning of the 2d. He should have abandoned all attempts against the Culp's Hill position. By concentrating his attacks from Cemetery Hill to Round Top, he would have increased the offensive strength of his line by at least one-third. In doing this, he would not have subjected himself to a dangerous enfilade from Cemetery Hill, because he had sufficient artillery to put that hill under cross-fire from Seminary Ridge and from Gettysburg. Lee finally discarded the plan of shortening his line on the representation of Ewell that Johnson could take Culp's Hill— an instance where the advantage that would certainly have resulted from a concentrated attack was put aside for the uncertainty of a *coup* on the flank.

The fourth reason for the defeat was the state of mind

of the responsible Confederate commanders. On July 2, [General James] Longstreet was disgruntled because Lee refused to take his advice for a tactical defensive. Determined, apparently, to force a situation in which his plan would have to be adopted in spite of Lee, he delayed the attack on the right until Cemetery Ridge was crowded with men, whereas if he had attacked early in the morning, as Lee intended, he probably could have stormed that position and assuredly could have taken Round Top. Longstreet's slow and stubborn mind rendered him incapable of the quick daring and loyal obedience that had characterized Jackson. Yet in the first battle after the death of "Stonewall" it seemed the course of wisdom to substitute the First for the Second Corps as the "column of attack" because its staff and line were accustomed to working together. Longstreet's innate lack of qualification for duty of this type had been confirmed by his period of detached duty. He was never the same man after he had deceived himself into thinking he was a great strategist. It was Lee's misfortune at Gettysburg that he had to employ in offensive operations a man whose whole inclination was toward the defensive.

Lee's Failures at Gettysburg

But this indictment of Longstreet does not relieve Lee of all blame for the failure on the second day at Gettysburg. His greatest weakness as a soldier was displayed along with Longstreet's, for when Longstreet sulked, Lee's temperament was such that he could not bring himself either to shake Longstreet out of his bad humor by a sharp order, or to take direction of the field when Longstreet delayed. No candid critic of the battle can follow the events of that fateful morning and not have a feeling that Lee virtually surrendered to Longstreet, who obeyed only when he could no longer find an excuse for delay. Lee's one positive order was that delivered about 11 o'clock for Longstreet to attack. Having done this much, Lee permitted Longstreet to waste the time until after 4 o'clock. It is scarcely too much to say that on July 2 the Army of Northern Virginia was without a commander.

The conclusion is inevitable, moreover, that Lee allowed operations to drift on the morning of the 2d, not only because he would not deal sternly with Longstreet but also because he placed such unquestioning reliance on his army that he believed the men in the ranks could redeem Longstreet's delay. If Longstreet was insubordinate, Lee was overconfident. This psychological factor of the over-confidence of the commanding general is almost of sufficient importance to be regarded as a separate reason for the Confederate defeat.

The mind of Ewell was similarly at fault on July 2. Although he had then been given his direct orders by Lee in person, Ewell either did not comprehend the importance of the task assigned him or else he was unable to co-ordinate the attacks of his three divisions, two of which were under commanders almost as unfamiliar with their duties as he was. Ewell's attacks were those of Lee at Malvern Hill, or those of [Union General George] McClellan at Sharpsburg, isolated, disjointed, and ineffective. Had Early and [General Robert] Rodes engaged when Johnson made his assault, there is at least a probability that Early could have held Cemetery Hill. If he had done so, the evacuation of Cemetery Ridge would have been necessary that night, or else [General George] Pickett's charge could have been driven home with the help of a shattering Confederate fire from the captured eminence.

Lee's Reorganized Army Fails to Respond

Fifth and most fundamental among the reasons for Lee's failure at Gettysburg was the general lack by the reorganized army of co-ordination in attack. Some of the instances of this on July 2 have already been given. To these may be added the failure of [General] A.P. Hill's corps to support the advance of [General A.R.] Wright and of [General Cadmus] Wilcox when the attack of the First Corps reached the front of the Third. General Wilcox maintained that [General Richard] Anderson's division was badly handled then and that the captured ground could have been retained if Anderson had been on the alert. Wilcox may have been in error concerning some of the details, but the impression left by the operations of Hill's corps is that they were not unified and directed to the all-important object of seizing and holding Cemetery Ridge. An even greater lack of co-ordination was apparent on the 3d. It was imperative on the last day of the battle that the three corps act together with absolute precision, for every one must have realized that another repulse would necessitate a retreat. Yet the reorganized army did not fight as a single machine. Longstreet could have had Pickett on the field at dawn and could have attacked when Ewell did; but he was still so intent on carrying his own point and moving by the right flank, that he devoted himself to that plan instead of hurrying Pickett into position. When Longstreet would not attack with his whole corps, Lee made the mistake of shifting his attack northward, and of delivering it with parts of two corps. Pickett and [General J.J.] Pettigrew advanced together almost as well as if they had belonged to the same corps, but there was no co-ordination of their support. The men at the time—and critics since then—seem to have been so intent on watching the charge that they have forgotten the tragic fact that after the two assaulting divisions reached Cemetery

The South's defeat was not the result of Lee's failed leadership, rather it was the adverse circumstances that surrounded him.

Ridge they received no reinforcements. Probably it was the course of wisdom not to have rushed Anderson forward along with Pickett and Pettigrew, but there has never been any satisfactory explanation why Wilcox's advance was delayed or the whole of Anderson's division was not thrown in when it was apparent that Pickett and Pettigrew would reach the enemy's position. It was probably to this that Lee referred, on the night of July 3, in his conversation with General Imboden. There were risks, of course, in hurling all the troops against Cemetery Ridge, and leaving none in reserve, but Lee had done the same thing at Gaines's Mill and at Second Manassas, and in both instances had driven the enemy from the field. Similarly, the advance of the left brigade of Pettigrew's division was ragged and uncertain from the moment it started, yet nothing was done by Hill or by Longstreet to strengthen that flank or to create a diversion. On the front of Ewell that day there was no co-ordination of his attack with Longstreet, or even co-ordination of his own divisions. Two of Ewell's divisions waited while Johnson wore himself out on Culp's Hill during the morning, and then, in the afternoon, those two in turn were repulsed. Ewell was ready to assault when the day was young, but Longstreet was not then willing. When Longstreet at last was forced into action, Ewell was half-crippled.

Lack of co-ordination was displayed in the artillery as well. So much has been written of the volume of the fire delivered against Cemetery Ridge that few students of the battle have stopped to count the batteries that were not utilized. Colonel Jennings C. Wise has computed that fifty-six of Lee's field-pieces were not employed at all on July 3, and that eighty of the eighty-four guns of the Second and Third Corps were "brought into action on a mathematically straight line, parallel to the position of the enemy and constantly increasing in range therefrom to the left or north." Nearly the whole value of converging fire was neglected. Furthermore, the Confederates lost the greatest opportunity of the battle when they did not dispose their artillery to blast the Federals from Cemetery Hill. That eminence stands at the northwestern turn of the long Federal line, the "bend of the fish-hook," and is open to attack by artillery on an arc of more than 200 degrees from the northeast, the north, the northwest, and the west. A concentrated bombardment on the 2d would have driven the Federals from

the hill and would have made its capture easy. Once in Confederate hands, it could have been a *point d'appui* for an attack on Cemetery Ridge. A short cannonade of Cemetery
Hill on the 3d, more or less a chance affair, played havoc
with the Federal batteries stationed there and indicated what
might have happened under a heavier fire. It is almost incredible that this opening was overlooked by the chief of artillery of the army or by the gunners of the Second and
Third Corps. There are only two possible explanations. One
is that General Pendleton devoted himself to reconnaissance, chiefly on the right, instead of studying the proper
disposition of the guns. The other is that the lines of the two
corps chanced to join in front of Cemetery Hill, so that liai-
son was poor. Neither Colonel Lindsay Walker of the Third
nor Colonel John Thompson Brown of the Second seems to
have realized to what extent the hill was exposed.

Southern critics of Gettysburg, admitting all these mistakes, have been wont to say that while each error was serious, the battle would not have been lost if any one of the
blunders had been avoided. There is a probability at least as
strong that few of the mistakes would have occurred if Jackson had not died and a reorganization of the army had not
thereby been made necessary. Then it was that Lee was compelled to place two-thirds of the troops under corps commanders who had never directed that many men in battle;
then it was that the sentimental demand of the South led him
to put at the head of the reduced Second Corps the gallant
Ewell who had never served directly under Lee and was unfamiliar with his discretionary methods; then it was that new
division commanders were chosen; then it was that the staff,
which was always too small, was divided among generals who
were unacquainted with the staff personnel, with the troops,
and even with the field officers; then it was that Longstreet,
by the ill-chance of war, was cast for the role of the irre-
placeable Jackson and became the appointed leader of the
column of attack, the duty of all others for which he was least
suited. Read in the light of the aftermath, the story of the reorganization of May, 1863, thus becomes one of the major
tragedies of the Confederacy and explains why the death of
Jackson was the turning-point in the history of the Army of
Northern Virginia.

Chapter 3

Was the North's Victory at Gettysburg Incomplete?

1

Lincoln Senses a Missed Opportunity to Win the War

Abraham Lincoln

President Abraham Lincoln was ecstatic when he heard that General George Meade's army had repulsed General Robert E. Lee's forces at Gettysburg. For Lincoln, the Union success at Gettysburg could be the major victory that would lead to the surrender of Lee's army and end the Civil War. To bring about that outcome, Lincoln urged Meade to attack Lee's badly damaged army as it retreated toward Virginia. In the series of letters to politicians and military men presented here, Lincoln first expresses his optimism that Lee's army could be destroyed, but later conveys his frustration that Meade had allowed Lee to escape across the Potomac River into Virginia. Having escaped total destruction at Gettysburg, Lee's Army of Northern Virginia would fight for the Confederacy for another twenty-one months.

Soldiers' Home,
[Washington,] July 6, 1863—7 P.M.

Major-General [Henry] Halleck: I left the telegraph office a good deal dissatisfied. You know I did not like the phrase, in Orders, No. 68, I believe, "Drive the invaders from our soil." Since that, I see a dispatch from General [William] French, saying the enemy is crossing his wounded over the river in flats, without saying why he does not stop it, or even intimating a thought that it ought to be stopped.

Excerpted from *The Collected Works of Abraham Lincoln*, edited by Roy P. Basler (New Brunswick, NJ: Rutgers University Press, 1953). Copyright © 1953 by The Abraham Lincoln Association.

Still later, another dispatch from General [Alfred] Pleason-ton, by direction of General Meade, to General French, stating that the main army is halted because it is believed the rebels are concentrating "on the road toward Hagerstown, beyond Fairfield," and is not to move until it is ascertained that the rebels intend to evacuate Cumberland Valley.

These things all appear to me to be connected with a purpose to cover Baltimore and Washington, and to get the enemy across the river again without a further collision, and they do not appear connected with a purpose to prevent his crossing and to destroy him. I do fear the former purpose is acted upon and the latter is rejected.

If you are satisfied the latter purpose is entertained and is judiciously pursued, I am content. If you are not so satis-fied, please look to it. Yours, truly,   A. LINCOLN.

• • •

Major-General Halleck: [July 7, 1863]
We have certain information that Vicksburg surren-dered to General Grant on the 4th of July. Now, if General Meade can complete his work, so gloriously prosecuted thus far, by the literal or substantial destruction of Lee's army, the rebellion will be over. Yours, truly,   A. LINCOLN.

• • •

Hon. F.F. Low.   Washington, D.C.,
San Francisco, Cal.   July 8, 1863
There is no doubt that Gen. Meade, now commanding the Army of the Potomac, beat Lee, at Gettysburg, Pa. at the end of a three days battle; and that the latter is now crossing the Potomac at Williamsport, over the swolen stream & with poor means of crossing, and closely pressed by Meade. We also have despatches rendering it entirely certain that Vicksburg surrendered to Gen. Grant on the glorious old 4th.   A. LINCOLN

• • •

Hon. J.K. Dubois   Washington City, D.C.
Springfield, Ills—   July 11, 1863
It is certain that after three days fighting at Gettysburg, Lee withdrew and made for the Potomac; that he found the river so swolen as to prevent his crossing, that he is still this side near Hagerstown and Williamsport, preparing to de-fend himself; and that Meade is close upon him preparing to attack him, heavy skirmishing having occurred nearly all day yesterday. I am more than satisfied with what has hap-

pened North of the Potomac so far, and am anxious and hopeful for what is to come.   A. LINCOLN

• • •

                                                    Executive Mansion,
Major General Meade   Washington, July14, 1863.
     I have just seen your despatch to Gen. Halleck, asking to be relieved of your command, because of a supposed censure of mine. I am very—*very*—grateful to you for the magnificient success you gave the cause
of the country at Gettysburg;
and I am sorry now to be the author of the slightest pain to you.
But I was in such deep distress
myself that I could not restrain
some expression of it. I had been
oppressed nearly ever since the
battles at Gettysburg, by what
appeared to be evidences that
yourself, and Gen. Couch, and
Gen. Smith, were not seeking a
collision with the enemy, but
were trying to get him across

Abraham Lincoln

the river without another battle. What these evidences were, if you please, I hope to tell you at some time, when we shall both feel better. The case, summarily stated is this. You fought and beat the enemy at Gettysburg; and, of course, to say the least, his loss was as great as yours. He retreated; and you did not, as it seemed to me, pressingly pursue him; but a flood in the river detained him, till, by slow degrees, you were again upon him. You had at least twenty thousand veteran troops directly with you, and as many more raw ones within supporting distance, all in addition to those who fought with you at Gettysburg; while it was not possible that he had received a single recruit; and yet you stood and let the flood run down, bridges be built, and the enemy move away at his leisure, without attacking him. And Couch and Smith! The latter left Carlisle in time, upon all ordinary calculation, to have aided you in the last battle at Gettysburg; but he did not arrive. At the end of more than ten days, I believe twelve, under constant urging, he reached Hagerstown from Carlisle, which is not an inch over fifty five miles, if so much. And Couch's movement was very little different.
     Again, my dear general, I do not believe you appreciate

the magnitude of the misfortune involved in Lee's escape. He was within your easy grasp, and to have closed upon him would, in connection with our other late successes, have ended the war. As it is, the war will be prolonged indefinitely. If you could not safely attack Lee last monday, how can you possibly do so South of the river, when you can take with you very few more than two thirds of the force you then had in hand? It would be unreasonable to expect, and I do not expect you can now effect much. Your golden opportunity is gone, and I am distressed immeasurably because of it.

I beg you will not consider this a prossecution, or persecution of yourself. As you had learned that I was dissatisfied, I have thought it best to kindly tell you why.

• • •

Hon. Simon Cameron   Washington City,
Harrisburg, Penn.   July 15, 1863.

Your despatch of yesterday received. Lee was already across the river when you sent it. I would give much to be relieved of the impression that Meade, Couch, Smith and all, since the battle at Gettysburg, have striven only to get Lee over the river without another fight. Please tell me, if you know, who was the one corps commander who was for fighting, in the council of War on Sunday-night.

A. LINCOLN

• • •

Executive Mansion,
Washington, July 21, 1863.

My dear General [Oliver] Howard

Your letter of the 18th. is received. I was deeply mortified by the escape of Lee across the Potomac, because the substantial destruction of his army would have ended the war, and because I believed, such destruction was perfectly easy—believed that Gen. Meade and his noble army had expended all the skill, and toil, and blood, up to the ripe harvest, and then let the crop go to waste. Perhaps my mortification was heightened because I had always believed—making my belief a hobby possibly—that the main rebel army going North of the Potomac, could never return, if well attended to; and because I was so greatly flattered in this belief, by the operations at Gettysburg. A few days having passed, I am now profoundly grateful for what was done, without criticism for what was not done. Gen. Meade has my confidence as a brave and skillful officer, and a true man. Yours very truly

A. LINCOLN

2
General Meade Defends His Actions in the Aftermath of the Battle

George Meade

General George Meade was placed in command of the Army of the Potomac shortly before the Battle of Gettysburg. At Gettysburg, he positioned his troops on the high ground along Cemetery Ridge and waited for the Confederate army to attack him. Meade's battle strategy was successful; he inflicted on General Robert E. Lee's Army of Northern Virginia its most devastating defeat. Lee lost about 28,000 men at Gettysburg and, after three days of bitter fighting, retreated southward to Virginia. After the great battle, President Abraham Lincoln urged Meade to attack Lee before Lee could cross the Potomac River to the relative safety of Virginia. Meade chose not to attack Lee, an inaction that brought censure from Lincoln and from military historians who have studied the battle. In a series of letters to his wife, and one to General Henry Halleck, Meade defends his decision not to attack Lee during the southern army's retreat from Gettysburg, arguing that Lee was "in a very strong position," that Meade's army was exhausted, and that it had lost key commanders during the fighting at Gettysburg.

HEADQUARTERS ARMY OF THE POTOMAC,
SOUTH MOUNTAIN PASS, *July* 10, 1863.
I have been so busy I could not write. You must depend on [our son] George for letters.

Excerpted from *The Life and Letters of George Gordon Meade*, by George Meade (New York: Charles Scribner's Sons, 1913).

[General Robert E.] Lee has not crossed and does not intend to cross the river, and I expect in a few days, if not sooner, again to hazard the fortune of war. I know so well that this is a fortune and that accidents, etc., turn the tide of victory, that, until the question is settled, I cannot but be very anxious. If it should please God again to give success to our efforts, then I could be more tranquil. I also see that my success at Gettysburg has deluded the people and the Government with the idea that I must always be victorious, that Lee is demoralized and disorganized, etc., and other delusions which will not only be dissipated by any reverse that I should meet with, but would react in proportion against me. I have already had a very decided correspondence with General [Henry] Halleck upon this point, he pushing me on, and I informing him I was advancing as fast as I could. The firm stand I took had the result to induce General Halleck to tell me to act according to my judgment. I am of opinion that Lee is in a strong position and determined to fight before he crosses the river.

I believe if he had been able to cross when he first fell back, that he would have done so; but his bridges being destroyed, he has been compelled to make a stand, and will of course make a desperate one. The army is in fine spirits, and if I can only manage to keep them together, and not be required to attack a position too strong, I think there is a chance for me. However, it is all in God's hands. I make but little account of myself, and think only of the country. . . .

• • •

HEADQUARTERS ARMY OF THE POTOMAC, *July* 14, 1863.

I found Lee in a very strong position, intrenched. I hesitated to attack him, without some examination of the mode of approaching him. I called my corps commanders together, and they voted against attacking him. This morning, when I advanced to feel his position and seek for a weak point, I found he had retired in the night and was nearly across the river. I immediately started in pursuit, and my cavalry captured two thousand prisoners, two guns, several flags, and killed General [J.J.] Pettigrew. On reporting these facts to General Halleck, he informed me the President was very much dissatisfied at the escape of Lee. I immediately telegraphed I had done my duty to the best of my ability, and that the expressed dissatisfaction of the President I considered undeserved censure, and asked to be immediately relieved. In reply he said it was not intended to censure me, but only to spur me on to an active pursuit, and that it was not deemed sufficient cause for relieving me. This is exactly what I expected; unless I did impracticable things, fault would be found with me. I have ignored the senseless adulation of the public and press, and I am now just as indifferent to the censure bestowed without just cause.

I start to-morrow to run another race with Lee.

• • •

HEADQUARTERS ARMY OF THE POTOMAC,
BERLIN, MD., *July* 16, 1863.

I wrote to you of the censure put on me by the President, through General Halleck, because I did not bag General Lee, and of the course I took on it. I don't know whether I informed you of Halleck's reply, that his telegram was not intended as a censure, but merely "to spur me on to an active pursuit," which I consider more offensive than the original message; for no man who does his duty, and all that he can do, as I maintain I have done, needs *spurring*. It is only the laggards and those who fail to do all they can do who require spurring. They have refused to relieve me, but insist on my continuing to try to do what I know in advance it is impossible to do. My army (men and animals) is exhausted; it wants rest and reorganization; it has been greatly reduced and weakened by recent operations, and no reinforcements of any practical value have been sent. Yet, in the face of all these facts, well known to them, I am urged, pushed and *spurred* to attempting to pursue and destroy an army nearly equal to my own, falling back upon its resources and reinforcements, and increasing its *morale* daily. This has been the history of all my predecessors, and I clearly saw that in time their fate would be mine. This was the reason I was disinclined to take the command, and it is for this reason I would gladly give it up.

• • •

HEADQUARTERS ARMY OF THE POTOMAC,
BERLIN, MD., *July* 18, 1863.

... The army is moving today over the same road I took last fall under [General George] McClellan. The Government insists on my pursuing and destroying Lee. The former I can do, but the latter will depend on him as much as on me, for if he keeps out of my way, I can't destroy. Neither can I do so if he is reinforced and becomes my superior in numbers, which is by no means improbable, as I see by the papers it is reported a large portion of [General Braxton] Bragg's army has been sent to Virginia. The proper policy for the Government would have been to be contented with driving Lee out of Maryland, and not to have advanced till this army was largely reinforced and reorganized, and put on such a footing that its advance was sure to be successful. As, however, I am bound to obey explicit orders, the responsibility of the consequences must and should rest with those who give them. Another great trouble with me is the want of active and energetic subordinate officers, men upon whom I can depend and rely upon taking care of themselves and commands. The loss of [General John] Reynolds and [General Winfield] Hancock is most serious; their places are not to be supplied. However, with God's help, I will continue to do the best I can.

• • •

UNION, VA., *July* 21, 1863.

Your indignation at the manner in which I was treated on Lee's escape is not only natural, but was and is fully shared by me. I did think at one time writing frankly to the President, informing him I never desired the command, and would be most glad at any time to be relieved, and that, as he had expressed dissatisfaction at my course, I thought it was his duty, independent of any personal consideration, to remove me. After reflection, however, I came to the conclusion to take no further action in the matter, and leave it entirely with them. I took the command from a sense of duty. I shall continue to exercise it, to the best of my humble capacity, in the same spirit. I have no ambition or ulterior views, and whatever be my fate, I shall try to preserve a clear conscience. I have received very handsome letters, both from Generals McClellan and [John] Pope, which I enclose for your perusal and preservation. I have answered them both in the same spirit as appears to have dictated them.

• • •

WARRENTON, VA., *July* 26, 1863.

I think my last letter to you was about the 21st or 22d, when I was embarrassed at not ascertaining anything definite in regard to Lee's movements. The next day, the 22d, I had positive information he was moving up the Valley of the Shenandoah. I immediately put my army in motion and pushed through Manassas Gap, where I met a part of his force. By the evening of the 24th I drove his force through Manassas Gap, and debouched with the head of my army into the open country beyond, in the vicinity of Front Royal, and having collected five corps together, expected to get a fight out of him on the 25th; but on advancing on that day he was again gone, having moved his whole army and trains (principally through Strasburg), day and night, on the 23d and 24th. Of course I was again disappointed, and I presume the President will be again dissatisfied. It is evident Lee is determined not to fight me till he gets me as far away from Washington as possible and in a position where all the advantages will be on his side. I hear from officers who have been in Washington that the President offered the command of this army to Grant, who declined it, but recommended Sherman. I consider I have done a great deal in compelling Lee to abandon the Valley of Virginia, where, but for my movements, he undoubtedly would have stayed, as he did last year, employing his army in gathering in the bountiful crops of that region, and sending them to his depots at Staunton and Gordonsville for use in the winter. As soon as I can get ready I shall move on again, and it remains to be seen whether he will make a stand on the Rappahannock [River] or behind the Rapidan [River]. Some people think they are preparing to abandon Virginia altogether, but I doubt this.

• • •

WARRENTON, VA., *July* 31, 1863.

I enclose you two letters recently received—one from the President to General [Oliver] Howard, who thought it proper to write to Mr. Lincoln, deprecating his dissatisfaction with me, and informing him I had the full confidence of the army. The other is from General Halleck, written voluntarily and without any particular call that I know, unless he has had repeated to him something that I have said. His letter is certainly very satisfactory, and places the matter, as I have replied to him, in a very different light from his telegram. Disappointment was a feeling natural to every one, and was fully shared in by myself. It could have been entertained without implying censure, but dissatisfaction implied a failure on my part, which I repudiated at the time and since. I have answered Halleck in the same spirit as his letter, thanking him for his kind feeling and good opinion, and explaining my position, and stating that personal considerations aside, I hope that whenever the President thinks I am wanting, or has another whom he deems better suited, I trust he will at once put me aside. . . .

• • •

HEADQUARTERS A.P., *July* 31, 1863.
MAJOR-GENERAL HALLECK, General-in-Chief.

My Dear General: I thank you most sincerely and heartily for your kind and generous letter of the 28th inst., received last evening. It would be wrong in me to deny that I feared there existed in the minds both of the President and yourself an idea that I had failed to do what another would and could have done in the withdrawal of Lee's army. The expression you have been pleased to use in a letter, to wit, a feeling of disappointment, is one that I cheerfully accept and readily admit was as keenly felt by myself as any one. But permit me, dear General, to call your attention to the distinction between disappointment and dissatisfaction. The one was a natural feeling in view of the momentous consequences that would have resulted from a successful attack, but does not necessarily convey with it any censure. I could not view the use of the latter expression in any other light than as intending to convey an expression of opinion on the part of the President, that I had failed to do what I might and should have done. Now let me say in the frankness which characterizes your letter, that perhaps the President was right. If such was the case, it was my duty to give him an opportunity to replace me by one better fitted for the command of the army. It was, I assure you, with such feelings that I applied to be relieved. It was, not from any personal considerations, for I have tried in this whole war to forget all personal considerations, and I have always maintained they should not for an instant influence any one's action. Of course you will understand that I do not agree that the President was right—and I feel sure when the true state of the case comes to be known, however natural and great may be the feeling of disappointment, that no blame will be attached to any one. Had I attacked Lee the day I proposed to do so, and in the ignorance that then existed of his position, I have every reason to believe the attack would have been unsuccessful and would have resulted disastrously. This opinion is founded on the judgment of numerous distinguished officers, after inspecting Lee's vacated works and position. Among these officers I could name Generals [John]

Sedgwick, [Horatio] Wright, [Henry] Slocum, [William] Hays, [George] Sykes, and others.

The idea that Lee had abandoned his lines early in the day that he withdrew, I have positive intelligence is not correct, and that not a man was withdrawn until after dark. I mention these facts to remove the impression which newspaper correspondents have given the public: that it was only necessary to advance to secure an easy victory. I had great responsibility thrown on me: on one side were the known and important fruits of victory, and on the other, the equally important and terrible consequences of defeat. I considered my position at Williamsport very different from that at Gettysburg. When I left Frederick it was with the firm determination to attack and fight Lee without regard to time or place as soon as I could come in contact with him. But, after defeating him and requiring him to abandon his schemes of invasion, I did not think myself justified in making a blind attack, simply to prevent his escape, and running all the risks attending such a venture. Now, as I said before, in this perhaps I erred in judgment, for I take this occasion to say to you, and through you to the President—that I have no pretensions to any superior capacity for the post he has assigned me to—that all I can do is to exert my utmost efforts and do the best I can; but that the moment those who have a right to judge my actions think or feel satisfied either that I am wanting, or that another would do better, that moment I earnestly desire to be relieved, not on my own account, but on account of the country and the cause. You must excuse so much egotism, but your kind letter in a measure renders it necessary. I feel, General, very proud of your good opinion, and assure you I shall endeavor in the future to continue to merit it. Reciprocating the kind feeling you have expressed, I remain, General, most truly and respectfully yours,

GEORGE G. MEADE, Major-General.

3

General Meade Moved Too Cautiously After the Battle

James M. McPherson

James M. McPherson, a professor of American history at Princeton University, is the author of *Battle Cry of Freedom: The Civil War Era*, *Ordeal by Fire: The Civil War and Recon-struction*, and other books and articles on the Civil War. In this passage from *Ordeal by Fire*, McPherson argues that Meade was needlessly cautious in the days after the Battle of Gettys-burg. McPherson points out that Meade had at his disposal 20,000 fresh reserves for combat and that General Robert E. Lee's army had nearly run out of artillery ammunition and had lost almost a third of its generals during the fighting at Get-tysburg. Meade's hesitancy to attack Lee allowed the Confed-erate army time to cross the Potomac River into Virginia and to fight Union armies for another twenty-one months.

[G]eneral Robert E.] Lee and [General James] Long-street worked feverishly to patch up a defensive line to receive the expected Union counterattack. But no coun-terattack came. The wounded [General Winfield] Hancock pleaded with Meade to go over to the offensive. But Meade, a careful, cautious man who had been in command only six days, three of them fighting for his army's life, was in no mood to take chances. He feared that his troops were too ex-hausted and disabled by casualties to take the offensive. It was true that the Union army was badly hurt, with 3,155

Excerpted from *Ordeal by Fire: The Civil War and Reconstruction*, by James M. McPherson (New York: Alfred A. Knopf, Inc., 1982). Copyright © 1982 by Alfred A. Knopf, Inc. Reprinted with permission.

killed, 14,529 wounded, and 5,365 missing—a total casualty figure of 23,049, more than a quarter of the 86,000 effectives in his army. The battlefield presented a scene of carnage unparalleled in the war, for thousands of dead and dying horses mingled with the dead and dying men. But Meade had 20,000 reserves who had seen little action in the three days of fighting. A more aggressive general than Meade might have used these fresh troops to spearhead a counterattack. The Confederates had been hurt worse than the Federals. They had nearly run out of artillery ammunition, seventeen of their fifty-two generals had been killed or wounded, and between 25,000 and 28,000 of their men were casualties—more than a third of the 75,000 effectives engaged in the battle.

Meade's Caution

Meade's caution did not end with the battle itself. After remaining in position during July 4, Lee's army began the sad retreat to Virginia in a rainstorm exactly one month after it had started north with such high hopes. From the outset [President] Lincoln had viewed the Confederate invasion more as an opportunity than as a threat—an opportunity to cripple and perhaps to destroy the Rebel army far from its home base. At the President's urging, General in Chief [Henry] Halleck sent repeated messages to Meade instructing him to "push forward, and fight Lee before he can cross the Potomac." Union cavalry harassed Lee's retreat and destroyed his pontoon bridge over the Potomac. Since the river was too high from recent rains to be forded, Lee was in a tight spot. Straggling and desertions had reduced his army to 42,000 effectives, while reinforcements had brought Meade's strength back up to 85,000. Yet Meade, personally exhausted and in an ill temper from Halleck's prodding messages, followed Lee slowly and hesitated to attack the fortified lines that the Confederates had constructed at Williamsport while their engineers worked with desperate haste to build a new bridge. On the night of July 13–14 the Rebels escaped across the river over their new bridge with the loss of only a few hundred of their rear guard.

When Lincoln learned of this he was inconsolable. "On only one or two occasions have I ever seen the President so troubled, so dejected and discouraged," wrote Secretary of the Navy Gideon Welles. "We had them in our grasp," said

Lincoln. "We had only to stretch forth our hands and they were ours. And nothing I could say or do could make the Army move." When Halleck sent word to Meade of the President's dissatisfaction, the testy general offered his resignation. This was a serious matter, for despite his slowness Meade had won great public acclaim for Gettysburg. An administration that sacked a general after such a victory would look foolish, if not worse. Halleck reassured Meade of the government's confidence in him and refused to accept his resignation. Lincoln sat down to write Meade a letter to assuage the general's anger. But the President's own unhappiness caused the letter to come out differently than he intended, so he never sent it. "My dear general," he wrote after congratulating Meade on his victory. "I do not believe you appreciate the magnitude of the misfortune involved in Lee's escape. He was within your easy grasp, and to have closed upon him would, in connection with our other late successes, have ended the war. As it is, the war will be prolonged indefinitely."

4

President Lincoln Expected Too Much of General George Meade's Army After the Battle

Bruce Catton

Bruce Catton, the prominent Civil War historian, is the author of the three-volume *The Centennial History of the Civil War* and other books on the Civil War era. In *Never Call Retreat*, volume 3 of his history of the Civil War, Catton discusses the Army of the Potomac's movements in the aftermath of the Battle of Gettysburg. According to Catton, President Abraham Lincoln demanded too much of General George Meade's Army of the Potomac when he ordered Meade to attack General Robert E. Lee's retreating army. Catton points out that Meade's army was too badly damaged and too exhausted from the furious fighting at Gettysburg to attack and that Lee's troops were in a strong defensive position near the Potomac River. Catton finds Lincoln's criticism of Meade to be hard and probably unjust.

The elation Mr. Lincoln felt when Lee was repulsed at Gettysburg owed less to the removal of a threat than to the conviction that Lee's army was retreating with its neck in a noose. On July 7, [General Henry] Halleck notified Meade that Vicksburg had fallen and that the President had said: "Now, if General Meade can complete his work, so gloriously prosecuted thus far, by the literal or substantial destruction of Lee's army, the rebellion will be over." The

Excerpted from *Never Call Retreat*, by Bruce Catton (Garden City: Doubleday & Company, Inc., 1965). Copyright © 1965 by Bruce Catton. All rights reserved. Reprinted with permission.

President was in no mood to rejoice over the recovery of lost territory. He wanted Confederate armies wiped out.

Lincoln Becomes Frustrated

The President's feeling of frustration began when he read a congratulatory order Meade issued after Gettysburg, inviting the army to keep up the good work and to "drive the invader from our soil." To Secretary John Hay Mr. Lincoln exploded angrily: "Will our generals never get that idea out of their heads? The whole country is our soil." (The Union was endangered, not because Lee's army was in Pennsylvania, but because Lee's army existed at all.) As Lee went back to the Potomac, Meade cautiously following, Mr. Lincoln grew more impatient, and when newspaperman Noah Brooks left to visit Meade's headquarters the President confessed his fear that "something would happen" to save Lee's army from annihilation. On July 14 news came that Lee's army had indeed escaped, crossing the Potomac at night on an improvised pontoon bridge and returning to Virginia bruised but alive. Brooks wrote that the President's "grief and anger were something sorrowful to behold," and Hay remembered the President saying: "We had them within our grasp. We had only to stretch forth our hands and they were ours." Mr. Lincoln wrote a sharp letter to Meade, then soberly concluded not to sign it and left it in a pigeonhole; but enough of his discontent got through, via Halleck, to make the testy Meade offer his resignation. Halleck calmed the general, the resignation was not accepted, Meade was given promotion to brigadier general in the Regular Army, and on the surface all was well. . . .

Lincoln Demanded Too Much

Mr. Lincoln may have wanted too much. Meade's army had had about all it could take. It had marched hard and fought hard, thousands of men lacked shoes, some of the best regiments were reduced to sixty or eighty men, and an Iron Brigade colonel said that the campaign now ending was by far the worst the Army of the Potomac ever experienced. Meade himself was living on nothing much more than a stern sense of duty. On July 8 he wrote to Mrs. Meade: "From the time I took command until today, now over ten days, I have not changed my clothes have not had a regular nights rest & many nights not a wink of sleep and for several days did not even wash my face & hands—no regular food and all the time in a state of mental anxiety. Indeed, I think I have lived as much in this time as in the last 30 years." He did not honestly feel that he had won a great victory; the most he would say was that "Lee was defeated in his efforts to destroy my army." He hoped to overtake Lee and defeat him, but in all of its career the Army of the Potomac had never yet made an energetic pursuit and it was hard to begin now. Meade was still new in command, some of his lieutenants were second-raters, the army was tired and he was tired, and almost in despair he wrote: "I *suffer* very much from anxiety & responsibility—I can get no reliable information of the enemy and have to grope my way in the dark—it is wonderful the difficulty I have in obtaining correct information—I *want Corps Comdrs.*"

Despite Lincoln's criticism, Meade (pictured center with staff) staunchly defended his decision not to attack Lee's retreating army.

When Lee at last reached the Potomac [River] near Williamsport, and dug in to await attack while his engineers were preparing a crossing, Meade found the Confederates well posted in a strong position. He consulted his corps commanders, found that hardly any of them felt that the army ought to attack, studied the situation at more length, made up his mind to attack anyway—and learned next day that Lee had crossed the river during the night and early morning, and that the last chance to strike a finishing blow was gone. On top of this came Halleck's messages indicating that the President and the general-in-chief were dissatisfied, and Meade told his wife: "It is hard after working as I have done and accomplishing as much to be found fault with for not doing impossibilities."

It was hard, and probably it was unjust: the one fact that mattered was that Lee had got away. The Army of Northern Virginia had not been taken off of the board, and Mr. Lincoln was no more interested in the reasons why it had not been removed than Mr. [Jefferson] Davis was interested in the reasons why Vicksburg had been surrendered. In point of fact, the Army of Northern Virginia had done well to get away at all. It had been hurt worse than Meade's army had been hurt and it had been weaker to begin with; all of the reasons that kept the Federal army from making a rapid pursuit rested on this army with equal weight; and yet somehow, on the march back to Virginia, Lee's army had found the extra ounce of energy that enabled it to move quickly in spite of exhaustion.

Chapter **4**

The Battle of Gettysburg in Context

1

Gettysburg: A Test for Democratic Government

Abraham Lincoln

On November 19, 1863, a few words from President Abraham Lincoln gave meaning to the great battle that had taken place at Gettysburg and to the larger war of which the struggle at Gettysburg was a part. Lincoln's remarks, which became known as the Gettysburg Address, were delivered at a ceremony dedicating a national cemetery on the Gettysburg battlefield for those who had died during the great battle. For Lincoln, the Civil War had become a test of democratic government—a conflict to determine whether government dedicated to the proposition "that all men are created equal" can survive. In Lincoln's words, the men who died at Gettysburg "gave the last full measure of devotion" to the democratic cause; they "gave their lives" to ensure that "government of the people, by the people, for the people, shall not perish from the earth."

Address delivered at the dedication of the Cemetery at Gettysburg.

Four score and seven years ago our fathers brought forth on this continent, a new nation, conceived in Liberty, and dedicated to the proposition that all men are created equal.

Now we are engaged in a great civil war, testing whether that nation, or any nation so conceived and so dedicated, can long endure. We are met on a great battle-field of that war. We have come to dedicate a portion of that field, as a final resting place for those who here gave their lives that

Excerpted from *The Collected Works of Abraham Lincoln*, edited by Roy P. Basler (New Brunswick, NJ: Rutgers University Press, 1953). Copyright © 1953 by The Abraham Lincoln Association.

that nation might live. It is altogether fitting and proper that we should do this.

But, in a larger sense, we can not dedicate—we can not consecrate—we can not hallow—this ground. The brave men, living and dead, who struggled here, have consecrated it, far above our poor power to add or detract. The world will little note, nor long remember what we say here, but it can never forget what they did here. It is for us the living, rather, to be dedicated here to the unfinished work which they who fought here have thus far so nobly advanced. It is rather for us to be here dedicated to the great task remaining before us—that from these honored dead we take increased devotion to that cause for which they gave the last full measure of devotion—that we here highly resolve that these dead shall not have died in vain—that this nation, under God, shall have a new birth of freedom—and that government of the people, by the people, for the people, shall not perish from the earth.

2

The Confederacy Lost the War at Gettysburg

Jefferson Davis

In 1881, Jefferson Davis, the only president of the Confederate States of America, published his two-volume *The Rise and Fall of the Confederate Government*. In that detailed history of the Confederacy, Davis discussed the impact that the Battle of Gettysburg had upon the Confederate war effort. In Davis's view, the battle was "the most eventful struggle of the war." Had the Army of Northern Virginia emerged victorious at Gettysburg, the South would have won the war, according to Davis. In Davis's words, General Robert E. Lee's devastating defeat at Gettysburg revived the North's "drooping spirit" and "impaired the confidence of the Southern people."

The battle of Gettysburg has been the subject of an unusual amount of discussion, and the enemy has made it a matter of extraordinary exultation. As an affair of arms it was marked by mighty feats of valor to which both combatants may point with military pride. It was a graceful thing in President Lincoln if, as reported, when he was shown the steeps which the Northern men persistently held, he answered, "I am proud to be the countryman of the men who assailed those heights."

The consequences of the battle have justified the amount of attention it has received. It may be regarded as the most eventful struggle of the war. By it the drooping spirit of the North was revived. Had their army been there defeated, those having better opportunities to judge than I

Excerpted from *The Rise and Fall of the Confederate Government*, vol. II, by Jefferson Davis (Cranbury, NJ: Thomas Yoseloff, 1958). Copyright © 1958 by Sagamore Press, Inc.

or any one who was not among them, have believed it would have ended the war. On the other hand, a drawn battle, where the Army of Northern Virginia made an attack, impaired the confidence of the Southern people so far as to give the malcontents a power to represent the Government as neglecting for Virginia the safety of the more southern States.

In all free governments, the ability of its executive branch to prosecute a war must largely depend upon public opinion; in an infant republic, this, for every reason, is peculiarly the case.

The volume given to the voice of disaffection was therefore most seriously felt by us.

3
Lincoln Gives Meaning to the Battle of Gettysburg

Garry Wills

Garry Wills, an American historian, has authored *Nixon Agonistes*, *Reagan's America*, and other works. In 1993, he won the Pulitzer Prize for his book, *Lincoln at Gettysburg: The Words That Remade America*. This excerpt from that text explains how Abraham Lincoln, on November 19, 1863, tried to give new meaning to both the Battle of Gettysburg and the Civil War. For Wills, the Gettysburg Address is Lincoln's attempt "to 'win' the whole Civil War in ideological terms as well as military ones." And according to Wills, Lincoln succeeded: "The Civil War *is*, to most Americans, what Lincoln wanted it to *mean*."

Not all the gallantry of General Lee can redeem, quite, his foolhardiness at Gettysburg. When in doubt, he charged into the cannon's mouth—by proxy. Ordered afterward to assemble the remains of that doomed assault, George Pickett told Lee that he *had* no force to reassemble. Lee offered Jefferson Davis his resignation.

Nor did General Meade, Lee's opposite number, leave Gettysburg in glory. Though he lost as many troops as Lee, he still had men and ammunition to pursue a foe who was running, at the moment, out of both. For a week, while Lincoln urged him on in an agony of obliterative hope, Meade let the desperate Lee lie trapped by a flooded Potomac. When, at last, Lee ghosted himself over the river, Lincoln

Excerpted from *Lincoln at Gettysburg: The Words That Remade America*, by Garry Wills (New York: Simon & Schuster, 1992). Copyright © 1992 by Literary Research, Inc. Reprinted by permission of Simon & Schuster and The Wylie Agency.

feared the North would not persevere with the war through the next year's election. Meade, too, offered his resignation.

Neither general's commander-in-chief could afford to accept these offers. Jefferson Davis had little but Lee's magic to rely on for repairing the effects of Lee's folly. (Romantic Southern fools cheered Lee wherever he rode on the day after his human sacrifice at Gettysburg.) Lincoln, on the other side, could not even vent his feelings by sending Meade the anguished letter he wrote him. A reprimand would ravel out the North's morale in long trains of recrimination. Both sides, leaving fifty thousand dead or wounded or missing behind them, had reason to maintain a large pattern of pretense about this battle—Lee pretending that he was not taking back to the South a broken cause, Meade that he not let the broken pieces fall through his fingers. It would have been hard to predict that Gettysburg, out of all this muddle, these missed chances, all the senseless deaths, would become a symbol of national purpose, pride, and ideals. Abraham Lincoln transformed the ugly reality into something rich and strange—and he did it with 272 words. The power of words has rarely been given a more compelling demonstration.

The Aftermath of Battle

The residents of Gettysburg had little reason to feel satisfaction with the war machine that had churned up their lives. General Meade may have pursued Lee in slow motion; but he wired headquarters that "I cannot delay to pick up the debris of the battlefield." That debris was mainly a matter of rotting horseflesh and manflesh—thousands of fermenting bodies, with gas-distended bellies, deliquescing in the July heat. For hygienic reasons, the five thousand horses (or mules) had to be consumed by fire, trading the smell of burning flesh for that of decaying flesh. Eight thousand human bodies were scattered over, or (barely) under, the ground. Suffocating teams of soldiers, Confederate prisoners, and dragooned civilians slid the bodies beneath a minimal covering, as fast as possible—crudely posting the names of the Union dead with sketchy information on boards, not stopping to figure out what units the Confederate bodies had belonged to. It was work to be done hugger-mugger or not at all, fighting clustered bluebottle flies black on the earth, shoveling and retching by turns. The buzzards themselves had not stayed to share in this labor—days of incessant shelling had scattered them far off.

Even after most bodies were lightly blanketed, the scene was repellent. A nurse shuddered at the all-too-visible "rise and swell of human bodies" in these furrows war had plowed. A soldier noticed how earth "gave" as he walked over the shallow trenches. Householders had to plant around the bodies in their fields and gardens, or brace themselves to move the rotting corpses to another place. Soon these uneasy graves were being rifled by relatives looking for their dead—reburying other bodies they turned up, even more hastily (and less adequately) than had the first disposal crews. Three weeks after the battle, a prosperous Gettysburg banker, David Wills, reported to Pennsylvania's Governor Curtin: "In many instances arms and legs and sometimes heads protrude and my attention has been directed to several places where the hogs were actually rooting out the bodies and devouring them. . . ."

Lincoln's Task

At the least, Lincoln had far surpassed David Wills's hope for words to disinfect the air of Gettysburg. The tragedy of macerated bodies, the many bloody and ignoble aspects of this inconclusive encounter, are transfigured in Lincoln's rhetoric, where the physical residue of battle is volatilized as the product of an experiment *testing* whether a government can maintain the *proposition* of equality. The stakes of the three days' butchery are made intellectual, with abstract truths being vindicated. Despite verbal gestures to "that" battle and the men who died "here," there are no particulars mentioned by Lincoln—no names of men or sites or units, or even of sides (the Southerners are part of the "experiment," not foes mentioned in anger or rebuke). [Another speaker at Gettysburg that day Edward] Everett succeeded with his audience by being thoroughly immersed in the details of the event he was celebrating. Lincoln eschews all local emphasis. His speech hovers far above the carnage. He lifts the battle to a level of abstraction that purges it of grosser matter—even "earth" is mentioned as the thing from which the tested form of government shall not perish. More than William Saunders himself, Lincoln has aligned the dead in ranks of an ideal order. The nightmare realities have been etherealized in the crucible of his language.

But that was just the beginning of this complex trans-formation. Lincoln did for the whole Civil War what he ac-complished for the single battlefield. He has prescinded from messy squabbles over constitutionality, sectionalism, property, states. Slavery is not mentioned, any more than Gettysburg is. The discussion is driven back and back, be-yond the historical particulars, to great ideals that are made to grapple naked in an airy battle of the mind. Lincoln de-rives a new, a transcendental, significance from this bloody episode. Both North and South strove to win the battle for *interpreting* Gettysburg as soon as the physical battle had ended. Lincoln is after even larger game—he means to "win" the whole Civil War in ideological terms as well as military ones. And he will succeed: the Civil War *is*, to most Americans, what Lincoln wanted it to *mean*. Words had to complete the work of the guns.

Lincoln is here not only to sweeten the air of Gettys-burg, but to clear the infected atmosphere of American his-tory itself, tainted with official sins and inherited guilt. He would cleanse the Constitution—not, as William Lloyd Garrison had, by burning an instrument that countenanced slavery. He altered the document from within, by appeal from its letter to the spirit, subtly changing the recalcitrant stuff of that legal compromise, bringing it to its own indict-ment. By implicitly doing this, he performed one of the most daring acts of open-air sleight-of-hand ever witnessed by the unsuspecting. Everyone in that vast throng of thou-sands was having his or her intellectual pocket picked. The crowd departed with a new thing in its ideological luggage, that new constitution Lincoln had substituted for the one they brought there with them. They walked off, from those curving graves on the hillside, under a changed sky, into a different America. Lincoln had revolutionized the Revolu-tion, giving people a new past to live with that would change their future indefinitely.

4

Establishing a National Cemetery

Frederick Tilberg

Even before the Civil War had ended, political and military leaders of the North realized that something fitting and proper had to be done with the Gettysburg battlefield, where so many soldiers gave their lives. The bodies had been hurriedly buried after the great battle by the citizens of Gettysburg, captured Confederate soldiers, and hired laborers. During the late summer of 1863, Pennsylvania officials planned for the creation of a national cemetery on the battlefield, a final resting place for the Union dead. The cemetery was ready for dedication in November. This excerpt from a handbook on the Gettysburg National Military Park, written by the historian Frederick Tilberg, describes the process of creating and dedicating the Gettysburg battlefield and cemetery. Almost a century and a half after the battle, the Gettysburg National Military Park continues to draw hundreds of thousands of visitors each year—individuals who wish to experience the place where the outcome of the Civil War was determined.

For the residents of Gettysburg the aftermath of battle was almost as trying as the 3 days of struggle that had swirled about them. The town's 2,400 inhabitants, and the nearby country folk, bore a heavy share of the burden of caring for the 21,000 wounded and dying of both sides, who were left behind when the armies moved on. Spacious rooms in churches and schools and hundreds of homes were turned over to the care of the wounded; and kindly

Excerpted from *Gettysburg National Military Park*, by Frederick Tilberg (Washington, DC: The National Park Service, 1962).

folk from neighboring towns came to help those of Gettysburg in ministering to the needs of the maimed and shattered men.

Adequate attention to the wounded was an immediate necessity, but fully as urgent was the need of caring for the dead. Nearly 6,000 had been killed in action, and hundreds died each day from mortal wounds. In the earlier stages of the battle, soldiers of both armies performed the tasks of burying their fallen comrades, but the struggle had reached such large proportions and the scene of battle had so shifted that fallen men had come within enemy lines. Because of the emergencies of battle, therefore, hundreds of bodies had been left unburied or only partially covered. It was evident that the limited aid which could be offered by local authorities must be supported by a well-organized plan for disinterment of the dead from the temporary burial grounds on the field and reburial in a permanent place at Gettysburg or in home cemeteries.

Creating a Final Resting Place

A few days after the battle, the Governor of the Commonwealth, Hon. Andrew Curtin, visited the battlefield to offer assistance in caring for the wounded. When official duties required his return to Harrisburg, he appointed Attorney David Wills, of Gettysburg, to act as his special agent. At the time of his visit, the Governor was especially distressed by the condition of the dead. In response to the Governor's desire that the remains be brought together in a place set aside for the purpose, Mr. Wills selected land on the northern slope of Cemetery Hill and suggested that the State of Pennsylvania purchase the ground at once in order that interments could begin without delay. He proposed that contributions for the purpose of laying out and landscaping the grounds be asked from legislatures of the States whose soldiers had taken part in the battle.

Within 6 weeks, Mr. Wills had purchased 17 acres of ground on Cemetery Hill and engaged William Saunders, an eminent landscape gardener, to lay out the grounds in State lots, apportioned in size to the number of graves for the fallen of each State. Each of the Union States represented in the battle made contributions for planning and landscaping.

The reinterment of close to 3,500 Union dead was ac-complished only after many months. Great care had been taken to identify the bodies on the field, and, at the time of reinterment, remains were readily identified by marked boards which had been placed at the field grave or by items found on the bodies. Even so, the names of 1,664 remained unknown, 979 of whom were without identification either by name or by State. Within a year, appropriations from the States made possible the enclosure of the cemetery with a massive stone wall and an iron fence on the Baltimore Street front, imposing gateways of iron, headstones for the graves, and a keeper's lodge. Since the original burials, the total of Civil War interments has reached 3,706. Including those of later wars, the total number now is close to 5,000.

The removal of Confederate dead from the field burial plots was not undertaken until 7 years after the battle. During the years 1870–73, upon the initiative of the Ladies Memorial Associations of Richmond, Raleigh, Savannah, and Charleston, 3,320 bodies were disinterred and sent to cemeteries in those cities for reburial, 2,935 being interred in Hollywood Cemetery, Richmond. Seventy-three bodies were reburied in home cemeteries.

The Commonwealth of Pennsylvania incorporated the cemetery in March 1864. The cemetery "having been completed, and the care of it by Commissioners from so many states being burdensome and expensive," the Board of Commissioners, authorized by act of the General Assembly of Pennsylvania in 1868, recommended the transfer of the cemetery to the Federal Government. The Secretary of War accepted title to the cemetery for the United States Government on May 1, 1872.

Dedication of the Cemetery

Having agreed upon a plan for the cemetery, the Commissioners believed it advisable to consecrate the grounds with appropriate ceremonies. Mr. Wills, representing the Governor of Pennsylvania, was selected to make proper arrangements for the event. With the approval of the Governors of the several States, he wrote to Hon. Edward Everett, of Massachusetts, inviting him to deliver the oration on the occasion and suggested October 23, 1863, as the date for the ceremony. Mr. Everett stated in reply that the invitation was a great compliment, but that because of the time necessary for the preparation of the oration he could not accept a date earlier than November 19. This was the date agreed upon.

Edward Everett was the outstanding orator of his day. He had been a prominent Boston minister and later a university professor. A cultured scholar, he had delivered orations on many notable occasions. In a distinguished career he became successively President of Harvard, Governor of Massachusetts, United States Senator, Minister to England, and Secretary of State.

The Gettysburg cemetery, at the time of the dedication, was not under the authority of the Federal Government. It had not occurred to those in charge, therefore, that the President of the United States might desire to attend the ceremony. When formally printed invitations were sent to a rather extended list of national figures, including the President, the acceptance from Mr. Lincoln came as a surprise. Mr. Wills was thereupon instructed to request the President to take part in the program, and, on November 2, a personal invitation was addressed to him.

Throngs filled the town on the evening of November 18. The special train from Washington bearing the President arrived in Gettysburg at dusk. Mr. Lincoln was escorted to the spacious home of Mr. Wills on Center Square. Sometime later in the evening the President was serenaded, and at a late hour he retired. At 10 o'clock on the following morning, the appointed time for the procession to begin, Mr. Lincoln was ready. The various units of the long procession, marshaled by Ward Lamon, began moving on Baltimore Street, the President riding horseback. The elaborate order of march also included Cabinet officials, judges of the Supreme Court, high military officers, Governors, commissioners, the Vice President, the Speaker of the House of Representatives, Members of Congress, and many local groups.

Difficulty in getting the procession under way and the tardy return of Mr. Everett from his drive over the battleground accounted for a delay of an hour in the proceedings. At high noon, with thousands scurrying about for points of vantage, the ceremonies were begun with the playing of a dirge by one of the bands. As the audience stood uncovered, a prayer was offered by Rev. Thomas H. Stockton, Chaplain of the House of Representatives. "Old Hundred" was played by the Marine Band. Then Mr. Everett arose, and "stood a moment in silence, regarding the battlefield and the distant beauty of the South Mountain range." For nearly

2 hours he reviewed the funeral customs of Athens, spoke of the purposes of war, presented a detailed account of the 3-days' battle, offered tribute to those who died on the battle-field, and reminded his audience of the bonds which are common to all Americans. Upon the conclusion of his address, a hymn was sung.

Then the President arose and spoke his immortal words. . . .

A hymn was then sung and Rev. H.L. Baugher pronounced the benediction.

5

Reconciliation: The Fiftieth Reunion at Gettysburg

Carol Reardon

On July 1, 1913, fifty years after the commencement of the Battle of Gettysburg, surviving veterans from both the Union and Confederate armies, along with journalists, historians, and political and military leaders, gathered at Gettysburg for a three-day reunion. The program featured a series of speeches as well as a reenactment of General George Pickett's fatal charge on the final day of the battle. In her book *Pickett's Charge in History and Memory*, Carol Reardon, a professor of history at Pennsylvania State University, describes the events of the fiftieth reunion. Reardon emphasizes that the Gettysburg veterans meeting again in 1913 "meant to celebrate the end of sectional bitterness." These men were understandably proud of their performance at Gettysburg, but any lingering bitterness had been wiped away during the five decades that had passed since they met as foes on the battlefield.

━━━

The 1913 anniversary celebration took place during a stretch of the hottest weather south-central Pennsylvania had seen in years. Crowds mobbed specially installed water fountains and the vendors of ice cream and cold drinks. The heat did not spoil the good spirits of the attendees, however; a young spectator admired the "wonderful double army of old men" who enjoyed a reunion that "might have been theatrical if it had not been so spontaneous."

Excerpted from *Pickett's Charge in History and Memory*, by Carol Reardon (Chapel Hill: The University of North Carolina Press, 1997). Copyright © 1997 by The University of North Carolina Press. Reprinted with permission.

With an eye to passing down to future generations the legacy of an honorable past, journalists took care to note the old soldiers' every word and action. The presence of distinguished visitors forged proud links to those long-ago days. Confederate generals Evander M. Law and Felix H. Robertson (son of the Gettysburg commander of the Texas Brigade) attended, along with Union general Lewis A. Grant. At a dignitaries' tent at the Lutheran Theological Seminary, a visitor met "two grandsons of George Pickett, undemonstrative lads of high school age," along with sons and grandsons of Generals Longstreet, Meade, and A.P. Hill. He could find no better symbol of national reunion than the moment in which a band played the national anthem, and all those "upon the dusky lawn—the Picketts, the Longstreets, the daughter of General Hill, the Meades, the long row of men in gray and gold—became silent, rose to their feet, and uncovered."

On "Newspaper Row," two tents had been set aside for the only woman permitted to have quarters in the encampment: Helen Dortsch Longstreet, the widow of [General Robert E.] Lee's "Old War Horse." A guest of Pennsylvania, she wrote commentaries on the celebration that appeared in over fifty newspapers across the nation. She sounded a discordant note, complaining at this late date—and despite her late husband's frequent comments to the contrary—that the battle's "famed charge was Longstreet's." Reportedly, [Union general] Dan Sickles had told her that "it is improper to call it Pickett's charge. It was made under the immediate command of Gen. Longstreet, who protested against it." Longstreet had told Sickles that "'I obeyed Gen. Lee's positive command, a command issued against my protest, for I knew that the charge would cost a useless sacrifice of thousands of lives.'" Now his widow "felt his dumb agony as he looked upon the marching columns and knew that it was their death march." No one seemed interested in taking up her case for historical accuracy, however; her pleas generally were ignored.

Almost any connection of the past to the present and future inspired the many photographers and journalists who swarmed the encampment. Hundreds of Boy Scouts who served as orderlies and runners listened for hours to the old soldiers' stories. "It is in the vital link thus forged between the passing and the coming generations that the great value of the Boy Scout contact with the veterans of the two armies really lies," wrote one observer. The reunion made it possible for the boys to enjoy the "heart-to-heart confidences of men who had faith in a cause, and showed their willingness to die for the faith," which "cannot but count for more than any printed page." One Union veteran who shared his tales hoped they would "take away the last excuse for the young people to cherish any sectional hatred."

A Spirit of Reconciliation

The spirit of completed reunion flowed through dignitaries' speeches. Vice President [Thomas] Marshall noted, "There is now no difference between North and South except cold bread and hot biscuits." Speaker of the House Champ Clark, who was eleven years old when Fort Sumter was fired on, told the audience how Gettysburg inspired his own generation: "Cold must be the heart of that American who is not proud to claim as countrymen the flower of the southern youth who charged up the slippery slopes of Gettysburg with peerless Pickett, or those unconquerable men in blue, who through three long and dreadful days held these beetling heights in face of fierce assaults. It was not Southern valor, or Northern valor. It was, thank God, American valor." A visiting clergyman, noting on July 3, 1913, that "it is to the minute just fifty years ago by the stroke of the clock since Pickett's charge came to an end," feared that too many Americans failed to understand the reunion's full significance: "Never before in the world's history have two armies that stood against each other like two castles with cannon shotted to the muzzle, met in friendship, good will, and with a common enthusiasm for the same flag" only fifty years later.

Only a few events disappointed the crowd. President Woodrow Wilson's address won few plaudits from some former Confederates who had looked forward to hearing the first postwar Southern president. Still, the address did impress an Ohio editor who recorded that the president's "clear, patriotic voice" could clearly be heard at "that sacred spot . . . the Bloody Angle, where the flower of Virginia veterans under Pickett went to their doom, carrying the hopes of the Confederate cause with them."

The veterans carried forward the theme of national reunion spontaneously. When one old Virginian got lost in the Union section of the tent camp, he met some of the veterans of the 1st Minnesota, which had helped to push back Pickett's men on July 3. He told them that he had served in the 28th Virginia. "That would be Olmstead's [Armistead's] forces, wouldn't it?" a Minnesotan asked. When the Virginian nodded, the Northerner asked with a gleam in his eye, "Comrade, what became of your flag that day up yonder?" "You Yanks got it, that's all I know," he replied. "Right! We got it then and we've got it right now," the Minnesotan said. "It's in St. Paul, you old son-of-a-gun, did you know that?" The Virginian stayed with them that night, and before he left the next morning, he admitted, "As long as some of you Yanks had to get that flag I'm mighty glad it was you-all. You-all are pretty good people."

The scene replayed itself in reverse as well. "Old Man Clark" from the Philadelphia Brigade found his way into the Virginians' camp. To some of Pickett's survivors, he crowed, "We saw you coming, and we licked you, didn't we?" They admitted, "Yes, you-all licked us, but we crowded ye some." "All right, we did it," Clark replied, "and, Lord God, how I like to tell you about it!" The observer who witnessed the exchange noted with pride, "What greater proof that the war is over is required than the ability to accept such badinage good-naturedly!"

A small contingent of men from the 111th New York of Hays's division took special pains to acknowledge that soldiers from commands other than Pickett's—without identifying [General James] Pettigrew's or [General Isaac] Trimble's forces by name—"also gave their bravest and their best." They had not forgotten "that upon their regimental and company rolls are also often written the words, 'Killed at Gettysburg.'" A few Southerners especially appreciated that this tribute came from a Northern regiment "which lost seventy-one percent of its number" in that same fight.

Pickett's Men

Standing out among the Confederate attendees, Pickett's men always attracted big crowds. Robert McCulloch, a veteran of [General Richard] Garnett's brigade and now president of the St. Louis Railway Company, told over and over how he and a "little knot wearing Pickett badges" met a group of Union veterans near the spot where "fifty years ago almost to the minute we had been almost as close to-

gether, but each seeking the other's life." Those badges—
each made of six inches of white silk about 2½ inches wide,
topped with a gilt strip and a star, and emblazoned with the
words "PICKETT'S MEN, 1863–1913"—became instant col-
lectibles. The seal of Virginia with the state motto "*Sic Sem-
per Tyrannis*" and "July 3rd, GETTYSBURG" finished off the
design. The Latin motto raised eyebrows, since John
Wilkes Booth had shouted those words at Ford's Theater
after he shot Abraham Lincoln, but, as Virginians quickly
explained, the motto had appeared on the state seal "long
ere Booth was ever born."

Edward G. Freeley, one of Pickett's men, drew a crowd
nearly each time he claimed to be the man who actually
"marked the highest place to which the spray of that charge
of Southern chivalry reached." He pointed to one special
spot and said, "There it is, right there, sir. No one got any
further than that, and there three of them beat me down
with the butt ends of their muskets." New Yorker Ross E.
Graydon spoke up from the throng around Freeley: "Comrade, I wouldn't be a bit surprised if I was one of those fel-
lows who banged you over the head, for I remember slam-
ming one Johnnie who had got out ahead of his crowd and
come romping right up here to the very guns of the battery
we were supporting." Peering closely at Freeley, Graydon
said, "Maybe you're that fellow—now, I wonder." Then the
two clasped hands and gazed out over the field together.

It somehow seemed appropriate that Virginian A.C.
Smith and Pennsylvanian Albert N. Hamilton chose to visit
the wall at the same time. In July 1863, Smith and some
comrades of the 56th Virginia had just climbed over it when
he was hit. He remembered that a Union soldier gave him
some water and took him to the hospital. With a catch in his
voice, Smith sighed, "He's gone to his reward by this time, I
reckon." Hamilton, a veteran of the 72nd Pennsylvania, arrived at the wall with a different group of visitors just as
Smith ended his story. He related how "it was right here that
a Johnny fell into my arms. I lifted him up and gave him a
swig of water, and then got him on my shoulders and carried
him off, but . . ." At that point, Smith—who had been lis-
tening—looked closely at Hamilton's face. "Praise the Lord!
Praise the Lord, it's YOU, brother!" he shouted. Then, the
"two old foes fell into each other's arms, embracing."

Naturally, all kinds of quaint items caught the interest of

the reporters. I.E. Tibben of the 71st Pennsylvania wore his wartime uniform, including canteen, knapsack, blanket roll, and "a big cap that must have been sweltering hot" that day. Virginian William H. Turpin of the 53rd Virginia made an even more striking sight with his heavy blanket roll and "the same old suit, the coat tied together with strings and his feet bound up in burlap bagging, instead of shoes," just as he had been dressed on July 3, 1863. C.P. Deering of the 28th Virginia, taken prisoner at the wall, praised his captors: "The Yankees were sho'ly very nice to us." He had spent most of the next two years at Fort Delaware, but even there, they "had the finest hospital you ever saw, and they gave us different stuff every meal."

A few of Pettigrew's men apparently slipped in with Pickett's veterans, but they won no special attention for their old command. Only a few individuals drew the reporters' notice. After an old Tar Heel veteran named John Caisan explained to a rapt audience near the Angle what he had done fifty years earlier, a man in blue interrupted to ask him to repeat his name. When Caisan complied, the Union veteran clasped the Southerner's hand. "What a singular coincidence, for my name is John Caisan, and I, too, come from Burlington, but it's Burlington, N.J., instead of North Carolina." One of Lane's men probably won few friends at home after a reporter printed a recollection of his fears going into the charge: "Boys, we aren't going to take it. It's too far across."

Soldiers who fought on other parts of the field clamored to see the site of the July 3 fight. "Interest centers about this, because the spot was accessible and well defined. It was the finish of the three days of bloody and fierce struggle, which in turn was the beginning of the end of the Confederate cause," wrote one reporter. "There is no American soldier—real soldier I mean—whether he wore the gray or whether he wore the blue, whose heart does not throb with pride at the valor and courage of his brother who made this deadly march and fierce fight."

Reenacting Pickett's Charge

The reenactment of the great charge itself helped to sum up for many of the attendees all the many emotions of the day. About 3 P.M. on July 3, 1913—as close to the minute, fifty years later, as they could surmise—crowds gathered to watch

about "500 all told, survivors of Pickett's Charge and the re-
sisting forces" line up to face each other once more. Picket-
t's men marched in double column, without arms, from the
Emmitsburg Road to the stone wall. The 24th Virginia's
Maj. William W Bentley, who was wounded three times on
that long-ago July 3, served as their commander this day.
Capt. T.C. Holland of the 28th Virginia served as adjutant.
As they advanced, spectators swarmed around Pickett's men.
Thomas O'Brian marched at the head of the column, carrying the only Confederate flag seen during the reunion. That
flag, recalled one observer, "was a history in itself—aye, and
a tragedy, too. . . . Nineteen standard bearers had dropped
in bloody succession beneath those Stars and Bars on that
awful day half a century before."

*The fiftieth reunion at Gettysburg included a reenactment of Pickett's
charge of the Union forces at Cemetery Hill.*

As they climbed the slope, they approached the stone wall
where fifty years ago had waited "the hated Yanks," and "behind that stone wall waited the Yanks to-day!" Maj. Robert
Stokes and his adjutant, longtime Philadelphia Brigade Association leader John Frazier, led the Union contingent.

One reporter described that final ascent as so steep that
some young men found it a hard climb, "but the old men
didn't seem to regard it as a difficult thing at all." Mark

Boone of the 57th Virginia, aged 78, reached "that ancient, disputed wall" first. J.L. Rockwell of the 106th Pennsylvania, aged 72, helped him over. Southerners clasped hands with smiling Northerners across the barricade. "Hand-grips! Hand-grips that spelled: *'One Nation; One Flag,'*" wrote one man. After the Virginians climbed over the wall, a few walked over to the stone marking the place where Armistead fell. "They were the men who broke into the Union lines with him and saw him die," explained an on-looker, and as they gathered around the little monument, Northern men stood in silence with them.

Festivities resumed when the Southern veterans broke out in cheers and the Northern soldiers quickly joined in. Pennsylvania congressman J. Hampton Moore greeted them: "You meet again here at the 'Bloody Angle,' the very zenith of the mighty current of the war, not as furious, fighting champions of State or Section, but as messengers of peace." He presented an American flag to Pickett's men: "With shot for shot and bayonet for bayonet you met each other then. Now you know, on either side, the foeman you met were worthy of your steel." At the wall, Capt. Robert Douthat raised up the Confederate flag again, "crossed it with the triangular flag of the Philadelphia brigade, and between the two emblems he planted the brand new *Stars and Stripes!*" The significance of the action was not lost on the crowd, and a shout of approval "fairly split the air." Each of Pickett's men received a bronze medallion bearing the words "Philadelphia Brigade" and "Pickett's Division," courtesy of the John Wanamaker Company of Philadelphia.

The stifling hot weather inflicted the only casualties this July 3. Several of the old soldiers collapsed from the heat and the emotions of the day. Most, however, just walked slowly back to the tent city, discussing a new plan "which has run like wildfire all over camp to-day" for a new monument "to commemorate both the first and the second charge of Pickett's Division."

Journalists Record the Events

Journalists, many of whom were too young to remember much about the war, found both the recreation of the charge and the following ceremonies impressive. "'Dramatic' seems an overworked and unsatisfying word when applied to the incidents that marked the week of the Gettysburg reunion," wrote one correspondent, who nonetheless assured readers that there "was no 'staginess' about any of the proceedings." A *New York Times* correspondent went to see if Meade's headquarters looked anything like the way Samuel Wilkeson had described it so colorfully in the aftermath of the artillery bombardment on July 3; he noted that "the hollyhocks and roses that Wilkeson describes are blooming again to-day."

Enterprising photographers got their share of contrived shots. By and large, however, the veterans themselves decided what was appropriate and what was not. When a small group of Southerners started across the field of Pickett's Charge by themselves, a man with a camera hailed them. The Southerners deduced what the photographer wanted, and "with one common impulse they raised their canes, turned tail and fled like a lot of scared rabbits, the dreaded 'Rebel Yell' reverberating down the hillside." The resulting photos had "plenty of action in them—'all rear views!'"

An End to Sectional Bitterness

Veterans of both armies wanted critics of the ceremonies to understand that they sincerely meant to celebrate the end of sectional bitterness. Two old soldiers bought a hatchet at a local hardware store and then literally buried it out near Devil's Den "to show the world that between North and South no bitterness survives." As explained by C. Irvine Walker of the UCV, the reunion was not meant as "a glorification of the heroic charge of Pickett's and Pettigrew's men, or the magnificent gallantry with which the Blue line of Cemetery Ridge repulsed that charge," but simply as a salute to the valor of the American soldier. As a correspondent for the *San Francisco Examiner* claimed with some historical inaccuracy but plenty of emotion, "We know that it is well that the cause which lost did lose; that it is well that Pickett's gallant, glorious, heroic men wasted all their valor against the guns of Doubleday; that it is well that it was the men in Blue and not the men in Gray who slept that night on a field of victory," all in "a necessary, useful, splendid sacrifice whereby the whole race of men has been uplifted." The American people required no further evidence of the success of national reunion. A Mississippian recalled a comrade who called the July 3 assault "the charge which saved the Union," and this "epigrammatic characterization of this valorous charge" seemed "to define in some degree the sentiments that swelled in many hearts."

He could have added historians and partisans of the Southern commands from states other than Virginia to the list of those who could learn from the mood of the ceremonies. "Fame has been kind to General Pickett," one visitor wrote. "Never mind the questions which the military historians argue." It did not matter that the supports did not arrive. It did not matter that Lee, or Longstreet, or somebody else, erred in sending Pickett's men forward from Seminary Ridge. Just the same, "all the States of the Union claim those men to-day, and the veterans of the North, no less than those of the South, pay them their tribute of admiration. The Old Guard at Waterloo, the Light Brigade at Balaklava, and Pickett's men at Gettysburg—these three. Are there any others?"

Still largely missing from all the panoply were Pettigrew's and Trimble's men or [General Camdus] Wilcox's and [Colonel David] Lang's troops. Tennesseans, Alabamians, Mississippians, and Floridians could not even share in the satisfaction some North Carolinians must have felt to read the *Cincinnati Enquirer*'s editorial: "Martial story contains no more thrilling narrative than that effort of the Virginians and North Carolinians under Pickett and Pettigrew" on July 3. Herbert Francis Sherwood of *Outlook* almost got it right. He had wandered through the Confederate encampment at the reunion and climbed to the crest of Seminary Ridge about where Lane's North Carolina brigade of Trimble's command had rested early on July 3. Sherwood described how Lane's Tar Heels deployed for the attack fifty years earlier, but he still called the assault by Virginia's name for it: "Pickett's Charge."

Diehard cynics still could find things to complain about. Even Virginians, who should have been entirely delighted by the proceedings, could find fault. Virginia governor William H. Mann rejected a suggestion that he host another great reunion planned for 1915. Such a meeting would coincide with the fall of Richmond and the Confederacy's surrender, and Mann opposed marking that event with any such celebration. "The Gettysburg reunion was an entirely different affair," he argued. "The spirit of Gettysburg was of friendship and of kindly relations," not a celebration of victory or defeat, and "any reunion which celebrated the fall and burning of Richmond would be woefully inappropriate."

Gettysburg Controversies

The golden anniversary also brought out those who continued to argue that too much emphasis had been put on George Pickett, his Virginians, even Gettysburg itself. After giving the great reunion full coverage, the editor of *Confederate Veteran* felt compelled to comment that he still believed that "thousands of others deserved like applause with Pickett's men at Gettysburg." It meant nothing that "the final test of human strength and courage was assigned to that Virginia division," since "Pickett's Division was composed of typical Confederate soldiers, and it was that command that proved the test." Mississippian G.B. Gerald of Barksdale's brigade recalled the ferocity of the day: "One of my officers said to me [during the bombardment] that he had never believed the story about the world coming to an end, but that he'd be damned if he didn't believe it now and that it was going to take place within less than fifteen minutes." He had admired the steadiness of the troops in the advance "sometimes called the charge of Pickett's division and at other times the high tide at Gettysburg'" but he thought the writer who had asserted that "the century trembled in the balance" went way too far.

Of course, cringing most as they observed the proceedings were thousands of North Carolinians. A few months after the reunion, New York artilleryman Cowan recalled that a delegation of Tar Heels had attended the celebration to strengthen their claim to being "farthest at the front at Gettysburg." A quick reading of Hays's official report convinced him that "the Claim of NC is unwarranted." He argued that "none of Hill's corps advanced as far as Webb's front in the angle, so Va., not NC was foremost there." The tunnel vision of combat precluded his seeing anything north of the copse of trees even fifty years later. Still, some could be swayed. A Rhode Islander wrote to a North Carolina friend shortly after the reunion that some artillerymen from his state "told me that two men of a North Carolina regiment lay dead at the wall evidently killed by the canister fired at the command of Sergeant Olney." He now believed that "the stone marking the high water mark as the farthest north that the confeds. reached on the field of Gettysburg is in the wrong."

Perhaps some of these comments reached Richmond,

where, in October 1913, the George E. Pickett Camp of Confederate Veterans formed a committee to consider formally "the facts bearing upon the presence and participation" of their general and his troops on July 3 at Gettysburg. The results could be predicted even before the committee issued its report: Pickett had served in "actual and active command of his division," they alone broke the Union line, and he deserved the mantle of "the hero and idol of the Gettysburg charge."

In the end, however, all the critics' gripes and complaints were ignored. Organizers of the great reunion did not set out to right the wrongs of history. Mostly, they succeeded in their main purpose: The celebration "forged the last link in the reunion of the North and the South, and wiped out the last remnant of bitterness and hostile feeling." Over the field of Pickett's Charge, "it would not be a great stretch of imagination to picture the heavens opened, and looking down on this scene the spirits of Abraham Lincoln, and . . . the great commanders and leaders on the Union side in this titanic struggle, and the spirits of Lee and Longstreet . . . joined in a perfect and eternal reunion in that world where war is unknown." The meeting had honored the nation, the fallen, and all those many veterans "soon to be mustered out of the army of the living and mustered into the army of the unforgotten."

As the veterans wended their way back home and the army packed up its tents—and many of its coffins, too, since only eight of the old men died—each American could find his own personal meaning in this reunion. John C. McInnis of North Carolina complained that "we boys always cald it Pickets newspaper charge[.] the Richmond Papers Blowed and it [up] and it has got into history but it is wrong. . . . Pettigrews lost more men than his whole Division[.]" But even McInnis would have to concede on one point: In the war for popular memory, in 1913 as surely as in 1863, Pickett and his men decisively won.

Chronology

May 15, 1863
Two weeks after his brilliant victory at the Battle of Chancellorsville, General Robert E. Lee meets with Confederate president Jefferson Davis and his military advisers and convinces Davis that the Army of Northern Virginia should invade the North. Lee's goal is to march into southern Pennsylvania and, from there, threaten a major northern city— Baltimore, Harrisburg, or Philadelphia.

June 3, 1863
Lee begins to move his army northward. His troops march west of Virginia's Blue Ridge Mountains, through Maryland, and, in late June, into the rich farmlands of southern Pennsylvania. On June 30, Lee's troops are camped north and west of Gettysburg.

July 1, 1863
Early in the morning, Union general George Meade sends toward Gettysburg a division of cavalry under the command of General John Buford to scout Lee's position and a large infantry force under General John Reynolds to support Buford if fighting breaks out. Buford's cavalry runs into Lee's troops west of Gettysburg. His troops dismount and face Lee's men along a ridge west of town. Reynolds's infantry arrives to support Buford's cavalry, and furious fighting breaks out. Advancing Confederate troops push the Union forces back toward and through Gettysburg. Union troops regroup and form a line of defense along Cemetery Ridge, south of Gettysburg.

July 2, 1863
At around four o'clock in the afternoon, Confederate troops under the command of General James Longstreet, after some delay, attack the Union's southern flank, anchored on the Little Round Top. Longstreet's assault is repulsed, with both sides incurring heavy losses. Near dusk, Confederate troops under the command of General Richard Ewell attack

Culp's Hill at the extreme north of the Union's line of defense. That attack also fails.

July 3, 1863

Early in the afternoon, Confederate artillery opens fire on the center of the Union defenses on Cemetery Ridge. But most of the shells from Rebel cannons overshoot their targets and land behind the Union lines. Union artillery pieces respond in kind. The cannons cease fire, and about fourteen thousand Confederate troops under the command of General George Pickett emerge from the woods to the west of the Union lines and commence a mile-long march over an open field toward the federal defenses on Cemetery Hill. Union artillery and rifle fire rip into the Confederate lines, inflicting heavy casualties. The Confederates reach the Union line in only one place, an assault that is quickly stopped. The Confederates retreat, leaving half of their number behind. Pickett's Charge is a devastating failure.

July 4, 1863

Lee prepares for a Union counterattack that never comes. He begins planning for his army's retreat into Virginia. The next day his army moves southward, closely tracked by Meade, but the Union general does not attack. Heavy rains slow Lee's retreat and prevent his army from crossing the Potomac River into Virginia.

July 13, 1863

After constructing a makeshift bridge, Lee's men safely cross the Potomac River into Virginia, ending Lee's Gettysburg campaign.

For Further Research

Books on the American Civil War

Bruce Catton, *The Centennial History of the Civil War*. 3 vols. Garden City, NY: Doubleday, 1965.

James M. McPherson, *Battle Cry of Freedom: The Civil War Era*. New York: Oxford University Press, 1988.

———, *Ordeal by Fire: The Civil War and Reconstruction*. New York: Alfred A. Knopf, 1982.

Geoffrey C. Ward, Ric Burns, and Ken Burns, *The Civil War: An Illustrated History*. New York: Alfred A. Knopf, 1990.

Books on the Battle of Gettysburg

Bruce Catton, *Gettysburg: The Final Fury*. Garden City, NY: Doubleday, 1974.

———, *Glory Road: The Bloody Route from Fredericksburg to Gettysburg*. Garden City, NY: Doubleday, 1954.

Edwin B. Coddington, *The Gettysburg Campaign: A Study in Command*. New York: Charles Scribner's Sons, 1968.

Kent Gramm, *Gettysburg: A Meditation on War and Values*. Bloomington: Indiana University Press, 1994.

Gerard A. Patterson, *Debris of Battle: The Wounded of Gettysburg*. Mechanicsburg, PA: Stackpole Books, 1997.

Edward J. Stackpole, *They Met at Gettysburg*. Harrisburg, PA: Eagle Books, 1956.

George R. Stewart, *Pickett's Charge: A Microhistory of the Final Attack at Gettysburg, July 3, 1863*. Boston: Houghton Mifflin, 1959.

Glenn Tucker, *High Tide at Gettysburg: The Campaign in Pennsylvania*. New York: Charter Books, 1964.

———, *Lee and Longstreet at Gettysburg*. Indianapolis: Bobbs-Merrill, 1968.

Garry Wills, *Lincoln at Gettysburg: The Words That Remade America*. New York: Simon & Schuster, 1992.

Books on Gettysburg's Generals

Freeman Cleaves, *Meade at Gettysburg*. Norman: University of Oklahoma Press, 1960.

Douglas Southall Freeman, *R.E. Lee: A Biography*. 4 vols. New York: Charles Scribner's Sons, 1935.

Alan T. Nolan, *Lee Considered: General Robert E. Lee and Civil War History*. Chapel Hill: University of North Carolina Press, 1991.

Michael A. Palmer, *Lee Moves North: Robert E. Lee on the Offensive*. New York: John Wiley & Sons, 1998.

Jeffrey D. Wert, *General James Longstreet: The Confederacy's Most Controversial Soldier*. New York: Simon & Schuster, 1993.

Memoirs and Diaries

John G. Barrett, ed., *Yankee Rebel: The Civil War Journal of Edmund DeWitt Patterson*. Chapel Hill: University of North Carolina Press, 1966.

Robert Goldthwaite Carter, *Four Brothers in Blue*. Austin: University of Texas Press, 1978.

Jefferson Davis, *The Rise and Fall of the Confederate Government*. 2 vols. Cranbury, NJ: Thomas Yoseloff, 1958.

John B. Gordon, *Reminiscences of the Civil War*. New York: Charles Scribner's Sons, 1903.

Arthur A. Kent, ed., *Three Years with Company K*. Rutherford, NJ: Fairleigh Dickinson University Press, 1976.

George Meade, *The Life and Letters of George Gordon Meade*. 2 vols. New York: Charles Scribner's Sons, 1913.

Robert Hunt Rhodes, ed., *All for the Union: The Civil War Diary and Letters of Elisha Hunt Rhodes*. New York: Orion Books, 1985.

Richard Wheeler, *Voices of the Civil War*. New York: Thomas Y. Crowell, 1976.

Websites

www.gettysburg.com   The national battlefield website offers information, pictures, and calendar events related to the battle and the local area.

www.nps.gov/gett   National Park Service web page devoted to the Gettysburg park. Some information and links are presented here for further exploration.

Index